DARKNESS FOLDING INWARD,
Light Emerging

DARKNESS FOLDING INWARD,
Light Emerging

by
Deborah Harmes, Ph.D.

Paper Paradigm Press

Dedication

To one of the biggest blessings in my life,
my beloved husband, Mark Harmes.

CONTENTS

Acknowledgements

To Mark, the husband that I so dearly appreciate and love, thank you for always being the most nurturing and understanding of men, especially when my head is in 'writer mode' and I am not always one hundred percent present in the room.

To Greg Calvert, my friend and editor for the last eight years—my profound thanks for your continual encouragement and excellent editing skills.

To Professor Angela Ruediger, my friend since graduate school—you have believed in this work and encouraged it with the biggest of hearts and you are an ongoing blessing in my life.

To Joyce Shafer, my friend from Chattanooga who paid attention to my non-stop nudging and moved to New York where she always belonged, your consistent friendship, encouragement, and skills are ever so valuable to me.

Finally, to the readers of my website and my books who have shared my life's journeys for almost twenty years, I thank you for your constant support and encouragement.

Introduction

*"We shall not give them fairy tales—we shall not give them
false hope to cling to or drama to distract them. They have
remained in the world of children for far too long."*

—The Dreamkeeper, July 2004

The prophetic messages of The Dreamkeeper have been
shared with readers and audiences around the world via the
Internet, lectures, and books for almost two decades. The
receiver of these visions and voices and the author of the
Dreamkeeper work has always been the sole territory of one
person, myself, Deborah Harmes, Ph.D.

My first book of prophetic visions, *The Dreamkeeper
Messages*, was published in 1999 (under the original title,
The Dreamkeeper) and for well over a year it was in the top
twenty books sales-wise on the Amazon.com website under
the category Alternative/Metaphysical. I have always tried
to be sensible and realistic about knowing that in sharing
my visionary work, I was writing for a specific niche market,
not the larger reading public. So that early success was quite
a pleasant surprise.

As the next five years passed and those prophecies begin
to unfold, many of those who had purchased the book or

read my then-frequent postings online began to write and ask if there was going to be a follow-up. In January of 2004, I released a revised and updated version of the book (just reissued in October 2009 as *The Dreamkeeper Messages,* 3rd Edition) that was double the size of the original.

While writing the first version of that book, I chose to simply take the visions that were given to me on faith and, in spite of my apprehension, to share them with the world. Five years later, I was grateful to be able to back up that faith in the validity of the work with pages and pages of proof gleaned from dozens of global news sources. But I was soon to find that she wasn't finished yet!

A year after the re-release of the revised book, the Dream–keeper began 'knocking' in my head again and she told me there was more, much more. But these words would prove to be even harder to write and the visions more disturbing to behold.

She never insisted. She simply asked if I was willing to step forward and share this type of news with the world again. This book that you now hold in your hand was meant to be published and out in the world several years ago. But a debilitating illness of two years, moving house several times, and my own reluctance to examine the issues that are presented kept this manuscript locked up tightly within my computer in an unfinished state.

Within my heart, the time feels right now and finally I feel able to share those visions and messages with the world. But it is up to each of you to decide whether to embrace or reject the material that follows.

"Backwards and forwards through time you go, learning and unlearning, remembering—only to forget again."

Be warned before you begin—this book is not for the faint hearted or those that long for a warm and fluffy ending. Some of what you are about to read will sound like a science fiction novel and some of it might sound like fringe-thinking or conspiracy-theory-nonsense. But no—it is none of those.

Many of the social, technological, global weather, and space changes that the Dreamkeeper told me about decades ago are now already well under way. As 'alternative' as my belief system might be to some people in regards to my work as a psychic, I am also quite grounded in reality and I feel strongly that relating these visionary episodes truthfully, without sugarcoating or softening them, is for the best at this point.

As fast as my sources (both the Dreamkeeper and visions from the collective consciousness) are giving me this new information, I am finding confirmation in the media. The rapidity of overlap between visioning and reading is rather jolting some days.

There is one further item to mention. Although there are quite gifted writers who take existing media reporting and then extrapolate a potential future based on what they have read, that is not how I work. My own method is actually the reverse of that. I see the visions in either a waking trance or a dream state and I document them. Only then do I get online or into the library to find source material afterward that backs up the visions. This has recently become quite a compressed process since, as I mentioned above, as fast as I am 'seeing' the future, confirmation is appearing within a breathtakingly short period of time.

The methodology of relating this future is also slightly different in this book. The last book, *The Dreamkeeper*

Messages, was told completely from the perspective of The Dreamkeeper, the being who has shared information with me since I was a child. In this book, I am the primary source since she now speaks through my own consciousness (for reasons that are disclosed later) without having to resort to either full trance or waking trance state. The three chapters that were dictated by The Dreamkeeper are plainly notated and you will notice that they have a slightly different 'feel' than my own writing.

I have also chosen to give the readers a bit more explanation of the nature of who the Dreamkeeper is and what my relationship is with her. This information will be a brief capsule summary of a much longer adventure that is detailed fully in my next book, a combination of autobiography and analysis of various types of psychic phenomena.

My previous book discussed the nitty-gritty of Earth Changes, how to prepare your bodies and minds for the times ahead, and what parts of the planet would survive in a more intact manner than others—so I feel that it is unnecessary to cover those topics again when the information of the first book is still valid. There are further challenges to discuss this time, but they are softly balanced by the Dreamkeeper's ongoing messages of love and encouragement for our species.

And so we begin a True Tale—not a Fairy Tale.

Chapter One
WHO IS THE DREAMKEEPER?

For the reader to understand the source of much of the information that I share with the world, a short explanation of the Dreamkeeper is in order.

She is a being not of our world—a life form from the beginning of time who has never resided in a corporeal state. Having no body has some distinct advantages though since she is able to traverse time and space, backwards and forwards, faster than I can draw breath.

Humourous, curious, and occasionally nervous letters have arrived in my email box during the past couple of decades—letters that asked me why the Dreamkeeper is visiting humans, what does she look like, and does she "take over" my body when she's here? But the most common question of all is one that has been repeated word for word on many occasions—"Is she an alien or an angel?"

No, she does not take over my body, and no, she is neither angel nor alien but something altogether different and quite amazing.

From very early childhood, a luminous and twinkling being appeared in my room most nights, dressed from head to toe in shimmering shades of purple. It was only many decades on that I realized that she gave herself this appearance so that a human child could find comfort in looking at something that was vaguely shaped like a human body.

This being was much taller and slightly wider than any human adult that I had ever seen and it was a looming though non-threatening vision to behold. Where there should have been a face and hands, there were fields of twinkling stars, and although there was no face for the being to speak from, I could 'hear' the messages in my head. Those starry fields at the end of her arms had no visible fingers, but I certainly could feel the gentle pressure of her 'hand' when she squeezed my small one encouragingly.

Having previously seen ghosts and angelic-type beings since infancy, she needn't have worried about whether I could cope with her arrival. From her very first appearance, it seemed like the most normal thing in the world to have this huge creature in my bedroom at night and I had no fear about her presence whatsoever. However, I did learn rather quickly to keep these visitations to myself when I discovered that other people didn't understand what I was talking about or told me quite firmly to just be quiet about all that 'imaginary nonsense.'

She arrived several times each week, just before I drifted off to sleep, and she shared memories of other lifetimes, stories of other worlds, and visions of the future by playing projections of those scenes in my brain like a set of private movies. Those nightly movies seemed more real to me than many aspects of my so called 'normal' life and I loved our time together.

The onset of puberty was traumatic enough emotionally and physically, but at the same time, I lost the ability to see the Dreamkeeper visually. From that point on she was a vision in my head alone and not something that was actually standing right in front of me in the room.

There are still times when I 'see' her in my head as she speaks and she looks nothing at all like the hooded figure of old. She is more like a glowing ball of light that shapeshifts according to the intensity of the message that she is transmitting.

In the mid-1990s, I gave a series of lectures about the Dreamkeeper messages to audiences both large and small. On several occasions she mentioned to whatever group that we were speaking to that we humans get 'filters' placed over our eyes at a certain point in our development and, much like the cataracts that the elderly develop on their eyes, those 'filters' prevent us from seeing clearly what is right in front of us.

As I got little older and moved into my pre-teen years, she explained that she was like a radio signal being broadcast to a single radio, and I was the one and only radio that was able to receive her broadcast. But she never answered me back then when I asked her why no one else could hear her.

You might have noticed that I refer to the Dreamkeeper as a she. That's because, as a child, I determined that her energy felt nurturing and feminine, almost motherly. So I have always called her a she from that time onward. In reality, the Dreamkeeper is neither a feminine or masculine energy but a combination of the two. She is an example of completeness and integration.

For as long as I can remember, I've had psychic visions of events that would come to pass in both the near future and distant future and as a child my attempts to share these visions with the adults in my life was neither welcomed nor encouraged. When the criticism and anger became especially harsh and difficult to deal with, the Dreamkeeper would reassure me that I was not wrong about what I saw in my head, it was not my imagination, and I certainly was not a naughty or willful child. Perhaps it was because I felt a complete sense of acceptance from her at all times, but it didn't occur to me to ask her who she really was or why she was there.

As I progressed through childhood, the teen years, and into young adulthood, my contact with the Dreamkeeper slowly faded and the volume on my internal radio was turned down to a very soft level. There was no dramatic severing of the connection between us, but the sensations were muted for many years. She kept her distance and quietly observed, but I could sense her there beside me as I married and enjoyed my adventures in parenthood.

Several decades later, my son and daughter were young adults living independent lives. During two tense years of health issues, I was nearly at a breaking point when I sat up in bed one afternoon, tears pouring down my face, and screamed out loud at the ceiling, "What do you want from me?"

And she was there—unseen but definitely there as the air felt like it was shimmering all around me and I heard her whisper gently, "Paint!"

Paint? I hadn't picked up a paintbrush in over 20 years!

The gentlest of movements in the air was like fingertips brushing my left cheek. "Paint. It will heal you."

And I did as she asked—slowly at first, but then with enthusiasm and gradually a calmness and sense of purpose settled over me and my health returned.

My life was fractured and incomplete on many levels by then and a divorce from my then-husband was imminent. I felt compelled to do something that was just for myself for the first time in a very long time, so I applied to several graduate schools and a few months later I began working on my Master of Arts degree at Goddard College in Vermont. Everything that had been topsy-turvy in my life immediately began to right itself and I could feel the old, optimistic Deborah returning to enjoy life, not just sleepwalk through it.

By my second semester at Goddard, it became clear that my topic of research was going to require several months of travelling throughout England, Ireland, Scotland and Wales. The Dreamkeeper was certainly with me on those adventures and now she was back and talking in my head non-stop!

While I was living in London in 1994, and with no warning about what she had planned, the Dreamkeeper added to our communications repertoire and began to give me long sessions of semi-trance-state automatic writing. These were so concise and deeply spiritual that I decided to take a chance on being considered a complete lunatic and I requested that my advising team allow me to include some of this work in my 300 page book being written as a Master's thesis.

After some heated discussions between various faculty members on campus prior to my return at the end of the semester, I was given permission to include the Dreamkeeper work in my thesis. Those automatic writing sessions are officially part of a Master's degree from an accredited university in the United States.

During that first year in England, I met Mark, the man who was later to become my husband. He was an essential part of the paranormal experiments that I engaged in that were radically different from anything I had seen or heard from the Dreamkeeper. There is another soon to be published book which contains the long explanation of how Mark and I met, fell in love, and got married amidst these adventures. That upcoming book also contains a more in-depth examination of the many beings that I have been in contact with throughout my life and offers a more thorough explanation of my relationship with the Dreamkeeper.

The Dreamkeeper sprang another big surprise on me in 1996 when she began to do vocal channeling while I was in a waking trance. Now didn't THAT make for some interesting bends in the road of a new relationship!

As I wrote my doctoral dissertation a few years later on the subject of Mysticism, she whispered valuable fragments of information to me and I had a broader appreciation of what those medieval mystics were experiencing!

For almost two decades, she has given me information to share with the world—words of encouragement, words of warning, messages of love and hope. But the reader may have the same questions that have crossed my adult mind at times. If the Dreamkeeper is this wondrous creature without the limitations of a body, a creator-being who is able to time travel to wherever she wishes, why in the world is she bothering to interact with humans at all?

She comes because she has hope for us as a species—hope that we will survive the trying times ahead. She comes because she knows that we are on the threshold of what she calls The Great Adventure when we finally depart from this planet for good. She has seen the many versions of humans and human-hybrids and she has watched as we brought ourselves to the verge of extinction on more than one occasion.

The Dreamkeeper has been a quiet bystander as waves of humans progressed to a point of being right on the cusp of an astonishingly balanced life that allowed spiritual and psychic and technological abilities to coexist and thrive. But each and every time, we unraveled that almost complete tapestry, were thrust back to a more primitive state, and had to start all over again. She knows that we are on such a threshold yet again, the door is beginning to open, and she is watching to see if we are able to make forward progress this time.

There is another reason for her presence in my life in particular. We share a link—a resonance pattern. When she says to groups that we speak to, "We are she and she is we," she is explaining that we have been linked throughout time because we literally are pieces of one another in different time-space resonance. That was a hard concept for me to embrace for rather a long time since it felt egotistical to even contemplate. I was deeply unnerved by that revelation for quite a while. But I am finally comfortable with it and am now able to flip quite easily between the two states of consciousness most of the time. It no longer feels strange or awkward.

She has chosen to split off a piece of her essence and inhabit, as an observer, the world of humankind. I think that it is one of the ways that she keeps track on how far we have or have not progressed as a species.

The publication of this book has been delayed for several years for one very specific reason and I take full responsibility for that. The source of the delay was me. There are now and will continue to be many sources of profound joy in life. Yet as thoroughly as I believe in that, many of the visions of the unfolding future, complete with sounds and smells, were so disturbing that I convinced myself that no potential reader would ever knowingly choose a book like this. However, since we have now entered the beginning of the period that she occasionally calls "The Pivot Point," I began to realize that I simply needed to get over my 'what would people think about all of this doom and gloom' and get on with the work of sharing what I saw.

I will not lie to you—it is not easy to see what lies ahead and writing this book has been intensely disturbing some days. Perhaps it is simply a matter of getting older and feeling the other side, the afterlife, in a more personal way nowadays that has shifted my thinking. But I have recently come to a much-welcomed calm sense of resolution about it all and I finally feel, once again, truly blessed to be a part of this work.

Chapter Two
THE TROUBLE WITH TIME

Amongst the letters I get from readers of my books and the web site for The Dreamkeeper messages, one of the most frequent complaints that I receive is that I do not give firm dates for the arrival of the various episodes that she sends visions of.

There is quite a good reason for this. Time is *not* a fixed thing! It bends and flexes, contracts and expands, streams and spirals in never ending movement. Someone having a prophetic vision of the future as they sat by their fireside in Europe 400 years ago would have seen one potential date for an upcoming event or events. But the subsequent years would have produced many variations and movements that could not have been predicted by the seer in that long ago time period.

I have had to face the fact that a vision that I might receive for a general time frame of a decade or two does not have an arrival date that zooms in on the specific day or month or year. And I do know and sympathise with the all-too-human desire to have things specified down to the tiniest detail.

Sorry folks! I certainly do understand your frustration with the process. However, I am able to outline progressions and patterns to watch for and then you will know that the event that has been foreseen is on the near horizon. That's about as specific as it gets.

I can give you a perfect example of something that occurred within the last few years. On the 26th of December in 2004, a 9 point earthquake struck in Indonesia and the resultant tsunami killed well over 150,000 people and left millions in a state of homelessness. I mention this because there is a painting hanging on my wall in the front hallway that depicts this earthquake and tsunami event in which I saw thousands of people being washed away. I painted it when I first had that vision 13 years earlier in the year 1991. I was living in Florida in the USA at that time but, even then, I knew I was not looking specifically at that coast. There will be a tsunami in the future on that eastern coastline of the USA, but the vision that I had as I painted that canvas was of foreign landscapes and villages that I had never seen.

When I had the first of the visions of Earth Changes in the late 1960s and early 1970s, I had a clear idea that they would be occurring near the end of the century or shortly thereafter. I tried talking to my family and friends about it, but back then no one wanted to hear about something that was 30 years away!

Try as I might, I do not truly understand or even get excited by time-space theories or quantum physics, so you may as well know that. Occasionally I will stumble across scholarly articles that are an exception to my previous statement, but they are quite rare and since my interests and academic credentials are not in any of the fields of science or mathematics, those subjects usually hold no allure for me.

My degrees are all in the arts, humanities, psychology, and consciousness and religious studies. And my brain just goes 'tilt' when someone—including the Dreamkeeper—tries to convey time and space concepts to me. I'm being really honest now and admitting that I memorized just enough science and mind-numbing mathematics to pass the required exams while I was at university and then I promptly forgot it all!

When the Dreamkeeper shows me the passage of time, she shows me swirls and spirals, a bowl full of spheres that look like soap bubbles, and ribbons floating in a cosmic sea of stars and inky blackness. She shows me bursts of saturated colour and there is a swooshing sound like a thousand voices sighing in unison in my ear. That is the nature of time for me.

She makes a quiet chuckling sound in my head when I ask for dates, or at least she used to. I don't even bother her with those questions anymore since she has always firmly stated that no matter how much humans might want it to be thus, time is not a fixed event. Time moves and so do those events in the future.

As I prepare to launch this book into the world at the end of 2009, there has been a strong shift by many of the world's most prominent quantum physicists toward the public admission that parallel world theories and time travel are now on *their* agenda as well. And with those revelations have come a closer alignment and occasional collaboration with those of us who have formerly been considered too 'alternative' to take seriously.

As to my own approach to the issues of time—for as long as the dreamscape movies are clear about the final result—I shall content myself with the swirling colours and the sounds of sighing and know that *that* is all I need to know, for now at least, about the nature of time.

Since the Dreamkeeper has been generous enough to share her visual projection method of teaching with me for so many years in a kind of 'Studies In Time-Space Reality For Dummies' I will give you a brief description of those visuals and place them in the context of how and when she revealed them to me.

The Slinky

In the autumn of 1994, while on holiday in Florence, Italy with my girlfriend Amanda, the Dreamkeeper showed me a visual image of time in the form of a child's toy—a tube of thinly coiled wire known as a Slinky.

In my head, the Dreamkeeper had shown me the rings of the Slinky pulled gently apart in a slightly separated position. This represented the way people normally think of time—as separate bands, each representing a year, a decade, a millennium.

This vision in my head appeared after Amanda had asked why I was able to stand in a historical place and 'see' a scene, complete with the people in their period dress, and I was attempting to explain it to her. The image sprang into my head and I grabbed a piece of paper and began scribbling a picture to represent the slinky.

If life in Renaissance Italy was only one band of the coil many layers down, and my current life was on a section of the outermost coil, what happened when, instead of being separated and loose, the coils were pressed together tightly so that there were no visible gaps. Could a person in contemporary time thus touch, no matter how briefly, the energy from one of those other coils? Were we able to 'bump into' other times and lives this way?

Ribbons of Time

The next description of time that the Dreamkeeper gave me was several years later when I was making fairly frequent updates on the Dreamkeeper website. This was prior to the publication of the first book and I was receiving rather a lot of correspondence asking for explanations of some of the concepts that the Dreamkeeper was giving me to share with the world via online posting. As I sat typing a response to one of my readers, the following image slid into my head.

I could clearly see the vastness of space and the twinkling of stars against the dark background. Suddenly, superimposed over the top of that background was a semi-transparent hand that was holding a bundle of ribbons. There were dozens and dozens of pieces of ribbon clutched tightly at one end in this hand, but the other ends of the ribbons were floating free and wafting in the breeze amongst the stars. Small sparkling dots began to appear on the swaying surface of each ribbon and the Dreamkeeper spoke in my head.

"Each of those dots of light is a period in time. See how they sit neatly on each of the ribbons? But what happens when the winds of time and change begin to blow them to and fro? Watch what happens next!"

As I sat there with my eyes closed, I could clearly see that many of the ribbons had begun to twist around one another and become tangled, knotted, or simply molded to another ribbon from another era in time. That partially explained my own personal interaction with other times and places while in dream states or trance states in historical locations and it also gave me a way to understand how history could mirror itself.

But why were we humans unable to progress, to learn from history and prevent ourselves from repeating the darker aspects of it?

The Dreamkeeper continued, "In many cases it is as simple as stubbornness or greed that allows humankind to conveniently forget the lessons of the past. But sometimes it is a matter of outside forces altering what your species is able to recall. For many of you the past seems like a long-ago and far-away place in time that bears no relevance to your fast-paced contemporary lives. But what if you were able to recognize that *some of the reason* that the world is not unfolding as you and your fellow humans could have anticipated is because the past and the future are *intentionally* being pressed tightly against the present time and those other points in time are influencing your here-and-now world. There are far more beings in your world than you could imagine who have the ability to cause alterations in the unfolding of time."

Many of us have noticed that the actions of world leaders, the forces of economics and social attitudes, the inclination towards war, and the extremes of deprivation or excess all contribute to a most realistic sensation on some days that one is living in the wrong time and place. Several years ago, back in the still-prosperous early days of the first President George W. Bush administration and months before the bombing of the World Trade Center in New York in 2001, I wrote an article which I posted on my website that shared my intuitive feelings that we were headed into a period of great limitations on personal freedom and a sharp economic decline. At the time I received letters from some of my readers around the world who asserted that I was being unnecessarily 'doom and gloom' in my approach since no such problems were on the horizon at that time.

Where travel is concerned there has certainly been a significant loss of privacy and personal freedom since 2001 in both Great Britain and the USA as all incoming and outgoing passengers on airlines are now subjected to a lengthy screening process and treated as if they are potential criminals instead of simply people attempting to get from point A to point B.

Quite strangely, the government of Great Britain actually prides itself on having the most 'observed' population in the world courtesy of an astonishing network of surveillance cameras that are blanketed throughout every city and village and are even positioned atop power poles in remote areas of rural farmland.

Both of the above examples, elaborate screening routines and constant monitoring of the whereabouts and behaviour of individuals, have a strong resonance of the widespread repression and watchfulness of Europe in the 1930s and 1940s.

Rings in a Pond

Moving on to another discussion of time, this is a slightly more elaborate version of the Slinky theory. If a single drop of water in a very still pond begins to spread outward in a ring, then multiple drops will create multiple rings. As they spread and the pattern of the rings begins to overlap, the lifetimes represented on each ring will also overlap.

This overlap can represent a greater theme of earthly time periods. But it can also apply to an individual and would offer a partial explanation for a clear memory of fragments of other lifetimes. Perhaps you have had episodes of bumping into one of your own past lives and that caused a recognition of and familiarity with places, modes of dress, or the emotional resonance of historical events that simply rippled through your body. It can be confusing to you if you have never felt any interest in a particular time period or place and yet when you encounter it, you are suddenly awash with unexpected emotions and sensations.

This has been my own experience in many locations around the world and I will be quite honest and say that it still catches me off guard for a few moments as these types of 'time bump' episodes unfold. There were literally dozens of these little surprises waiting for me as I travelled through Europe, a handful of them in Mexico, and a very few of them here in Australia.

Interestingly, the strongest 'time bumps' in the USA were all in the deep South in New Orleans, at a crumbling plantation in Mississippi, traversing the streets of St. Augustine, and in lovely old Savannah. Many of those 'bumps' were a bit uncomfortable as I remembered unpleasant aspects of other lifetimes. Yet there were many occasions when I was awash with memory, melancholy, and even a sense of how small or large my body was or the colour my skin and that gave me an answer to why I kept being drawn back again and again to live in the southern states.

Curiously, in this lifetime I have never lived in any of those places that I just listed and I eagerly waited to find *any* sign of a 'time bump' in the places where I did reside—in Louisville or Lexington or Berea in Kentucky, in Tennessee, in South Carolina, or in any of the many cities outside of St. Augustine in Florida where I lived.

A Bowl of Bubbles

The final illustration of the nature of time is one that has made me question whether the lives that we bump into in some locales around the world are our own, are only partly our own, or are the memories of someone else, memories that were so strongly imprinted on the place that we are able to step into the space and be coated with that residual energy.

In my own case, I have been doing this sort of psychic sensing since childhood and I am quite able to determine the 'edges' of each experience and know whether it is truly mine or an echo of someone else's life. Many times I have stepped into a spot in some abbey ruin in England or Ireland, for example, and I have been infused with the memories of the cold, the damp, the terrible food, the constant physical fatigue, and on many occasions the sense of hopeless resignation. But in each of those instances I've been able to say to myself, or to Mark if he was with me, "That isn't my life that I just walked into."

I have prefaced this final visual example of time with the remarks above so that the reader will take the time to analyse the episode a bit if they should happen to experience their own 'time bump.'

Picture a very large, very clear bowl that is filled to overflowing with soap bubbles. The bowl of bubbles represents the seething movement of time and space in the great beyond and each of those soap bubbles represents, in this first illustration, an individual lifetime lived by one person. Now gaze deeply into that bowl and what do you begin to notice?

As the soap bubbles glisten and wobble in the light, try to just focus on one small area and know that the same thing is happening throughout the bowl. Bubbles begin to bump into one another and as some of them stay completely intact, others begin to stretch and flex and blend into the one next to it, thus forming a slightly larger mass. Even in the ones that stay intact as solo bubbles, notice just how many sides are being touched by the surrounding ones. That surface contact can pass on knowledge or memories from the neighbouring bubble. Just how many lifetimes do you think that we have, share, reshape, or bump into in each of our own here-and-now lifetimes?

Now we will rename them time periods. Just as in the "ribbons of time" example, the decades, centuries, millennia contained in each soap bubble are bumping, blending, merging and even if they happen to retain their shape, their many-sided surface is passing on information to the neighbouring time bubbles that they bump up against.

Time repeats and repeats and repeats. We continue to engage in the same actions and attitudes that our ancestors did albeit with more sophisticated technology surrounding us. If I had been living (as I seem to remember doing) in the 1930s in Europe, I would have been pouring my thoughts out with a fountain pen furiously scribbling on sheets of paper. I must admit that a laptop is an easier option. But the emotions and conclusions that I am drawing about our early 21st century feel far too familiar—as if I should be wearing a bias cut tweed skirt with a cashmere twin-set and pearls whilst refilling that deep blue pen from an inkwell filled with peacock blue ink.

Do these multiple-surface contacts also help to explain why a person can have memories of living in time periods that overlap? As an example, I have a strong recall of a life in the 1930s as an adult in London, yet I also have an intense set of memories of dying as a child in the late 1930s or early 1940s in Germany. If we operate strictly from the conventional explanations of time, shouldn't such an overlap be logically impossible?

Writers of science fiction have long used parallel universes or parallel realities as a component of their work, but many in the population at large are unaware that this so-called fiction is actually based on scientific principles that go back over half a century. These principles of physics are now evolving at a breathtaking rate and they may answer many of my own questions.

After the Dreamkeeper showed me the huge glass bowl of soap bubbles, I decided to seek out some explanations and I was looking for examples that were easy to comprehend by a non-science reader such as myself. I was fortunate when my search engine turned up a vast list of credible sources. These included a documentary that was aired on BBC2 in Great Britain on the 14th of February, 2002 on a show called *Horizon*. The episode on that date was entitled "Parallel Universes."

This was the very first link that I clicked on, so imagine my surprise when I read the following paragraph.

It all started when superstring theory, hyperspace and dark matter made physicists realise that the three dimensions we thought described the Universe weren't enough. There are actually 11 dimensions. By the time they had finished they'd come to the conclusion that our Universe is just one bubble among an infinite number of membranous bubbles which ripple as they wobble through the eleventh dimension. [1]

Plainly the 'bubbles theory' has been around for awhile even if I had never heard of it prior to now! And this article about the BBC production is but one of many which give the latest theories from prominent physicists worldwide. A complete written transcript of the documentary is available at the BBC site and it contains further tantalising snippets.

Mainstream news publications such as *The Telegraph* in Great Britain are also covering these stories. In Roger Highfield's 21 September 2007 article titled "Parallel universe proof boosts time travel hopes" he states —

Parallel universes really do exist, according to a mathematical discovery by Oxford scientists that sweeps away one of the key objections to the mind boggling and controversial idea.

The work has wider implications since the idea of parallel universes sidesteps one of the key problems with time travel. Every since it was given serious lab cred in 1949 by the great logician Kurt Godel, many eminent physicists have argued against time travel because it undermines ideas of cause and effect to create paradoxes: a time traveller could go back to kill his grandfather so that he is never born in the first place.[2]

It was always interesting to notice that metaphysically inclined people, who may or may not have ever had any background in science or physics, have been stating for years that there are many universes, not just the one that we currently reside in. Yet the world of academic and research science seems to have been, until recently, a bit reluctant to tell the public via non-academic and more general-reading publications that they too believe the same thing.

There is one other area to address when we look at the final example of the time bubbles. If a strong, sharp 'event' of some kind were to happen in one bubble, surely it would have repercussions in the neighbouring ones. In our own recent history, I would think that the atomic bomb detonations at the end of World War II and into the Cold War period would certainly qualify as 'events' that made our neighbouring bubbles take notice. Perhaps that is one explanation of why we began to see more UFOs in our skies from that point onward. Perhaps the citizens of neighbouring bubbles decided to traverse the thin membrane that separates us to find out what in the world we were up to.

And what of any large scale loss of life in a single event or period such as a war, a plague, or a natural disaster? There seems to be a strong uptick in the reporting of beings of light, psychic communication with unseen beings, and angelic sightings during those periods of intense stress for humans. If one single body is able to emit a wave of emotional energy in times of danger or stress that is so strong that those that they love can pick up on it telepathically, imagine the non-auditory wave of sound that would be given off in the form of a tsunami of distress that would impact the surrounding bubbles.

Consider a few more things. What if those bubbles of time-energy were being manipulated in form, function, and energy-intent to enable an easy control over 'the masses' worldwide. I strongly believe that there are many examples of contemporary events that suddenly mirror events in the past and these are being intentionally created by energy-field devices. Plainly having those 'events' suddenly arise as attention focusers would get us so caught up in the unfolding dramas on our doorsteps that we might fail to notice the energy changes and evolution in our human bodies and spirits.

There are events on our horizon that will require a great deal of adjustment in our 'normal' view of the world and as these events arrive and we realise that other worlds were always a mere breath away from us, it would benefit our species greatly if we knew that we had options *other than* to live on an irreparably damaged world or simply step outside of our bodies and pass into the Great Oneness.

The artificial concept of death is one that I discussed in the previous book. But the option other than death and movement back into immortal realms that I am speaking about now would require the knowledge of and ability to transcend this particular Earth dimension *while still being in a state of mortal life*. There are already people on this planet who know how to 'step out' of their body and go elsewhere should the need arise, but many more of us were supposed to have had that ability by this point. That knowledge has been suppressed so that only a select few have access to it.

In spite of the needless distractions, artificial world-dramas, and suppression through fear, our bodies and energy fields are continuing to evolve and the global puppet masters are frantically hoping that by keeping us overwhelmed with spurious information and dumbed-down 'entertainment', we will ignore the wonderful messages that we are receiving from the Great Oneness about who and what we now have the potential to be.

Reincarnation Regression

Over the last fifteen years or so, many of my readers or lecture attendees have asked me about the value of doing a backwards examination of your soul life, a regression that is facilitated by hypnosis, to find out where you lived in other time periods and who or what you were in that era.

I do actually have personal experience with this since I tried a hypnotic regression once out of curiosity about twenty years ago and yes, it was quite fascinating. But if you asked me to give you a truthful answer as to the overall usefulness or insight that I derived from that evening, I would have to say that the novelty value was high but the level of helpfulness was low. The one positive thing that I did bring away from the session was that I had a clearer understanding of a spontaneous memory that I'd had when I rambled through the ruins of a medieval monastery in Ireland. It was a fleeting moment of insight that I could have just as easily had in a deep meditation.

Since I have training as a psychologist, I am quite able to recommend hypnotherapy for a variety of reasons and I consider it to be a valuable modality in therapy for everything from pain management to behaviour modification. I also agree that regression has been an indispensable tool for psychologists who have studied near-death recall, for example.

But the types of regression that I am concerned about are aimed at discovering the most basic of information—who were you in a past life, what country did you live in, how old were you, and how did you die. None of these types of sessions should be conducted by gifted amateurs, no matter how well meaning, but are best left to qualified psychologists or licensed hypnotherapists who are well trained in what type of side effects and emotional reactions to expect during hypnotherapy.

Moreover, in light of the earlier discussion of time as related to the 'soap bubbles' or 'water rings' theories, my other concern is that any past life regression will only ever give you a tiny glimpse into the greater whole of who you were in any one lifetime.

I am well aware that there are many of you who believe that it is helpful to know the specifics of past lives so that you may resolve any wrongs that you did to others in the past. If that is your reason for seeking out this type of information, please be assured that you have lived so many thousands of lives since your original soul creation, being the abuser in some lives, being the abused in others, having no knowledge of self-awareness in a great many of them, that it is an exercise in futility to attempt to rectify those other lifetimes. They are gone, they are not the here and now, and you are simply stalling and blocking your progress in this lifetime if you continue to obsess about the past.

But what of those religious or spiritual beliefs that claim that you can undo your debts or make an advanced payment towards hell-avoidance through your karmic-repayment actions in this current lifetime?

I encourage you to know that the Creator Force is not that small minded! Undoing past life behaviour or making a forward payment on a 'Get Out of Hell Free' card are control mechanisms that are *created by humans* to keep other more vulnerable ones under their thumb.

Please believe that this soul life that you continue to explore is not weighed or measured in such a primitive manner. There are no score cards, no tests are administered, and there is no Book of Judgement waiting to be read when you depart this Earthly existence. This is an interpretation that is both flawed and cruel and which is meant to keep you in a state of control and obedience.

Resonance is what matters—not the resonance of the past unless it is the rare and pure energy of love and enlightenment that has trickled down through the ages—but the resonance of the present. In this here-and-now time, you are able to remake yourself and recreate your life in any manner which you wish. On any day and in any hour, you can begin again with a fresh slate simply by acknowledging that your thoughts and actions have not served you well and that you now wish for a life filled with joy and compassion and love and abundance. It is just that simple!

If you persist in the belief that you carry forward the damage and anger and burden of actions that you may have done in other lifetimes, or of actions which were done to you, how does that help you succeed in this one? You are simply diluting your possibilities for drinking from the well of joy and goodness in this life. You are ceasing any forward progress in your soul life by maintaining too strong a contact with a past that is long gone and no longer applicable to the current time.

Chapter Three
EVERY BODY SINGS OFF KEY

From The Dreamkeeper

We have returned to the woman who is Deborah to give her further information on the years ahead so that you may make choices that are appropriate for you and your loved ones.

To answer the question that we are asked by many of you—yes, there is a heaven. It is not the fanciful creation of human minds and it is quite real. It resides in the same place that you now reside. It is around you and you are within it at all times. What you think of as heaven is just another version of your eternal life force residing in a different time and space reality. Yet you are unable to communicate with that other place except through dreams and visions. It was not always thus.

At an earlier stage of human-time, when the refinements had been completed on what was to be the human species, there were several thousand souls residing in each colony. In those first generations, those souls, who wore the outer shells of human skin very lightly, knew with every breath how to simply stop for a microsecond and speak wordlessly to whoever/whatever surrounded them on the other side of the breath-thin incarnation-veil that separates you. This awareness and ability, which was part of your original soul heritage, was soon to pass into a state of distant memory.

In some cases the memory loss and resultant state of separation was done intentionally by the races of off-planetary 'gods' who resided amongst you in those early days. These 'gods' took the original beings and altered the appearance, brain encoding, and memories so that humans would not remember their connection with the source of us all, the Oneness. It was a selfish and highly successful act with one goal that has resonated throughout the ages—to keep you in a state of ignorant servitude and to keep you unaware of how they manipulate time and space for their own purposes.

We know full well how they operated since we Dream-keepers were one of many Creator species that acted on behalf of the Oneness when, in a distant part of early time, we created those races of 'gods' who came to Earth at a later time and made you humans.

Having launched the 'god' races, we stepped back and moved on to other tasks. But as time passed and the new young 'god' races grew, prospered, and travelled out into space to create and then repeatedly refine their various versions of manufactured humankind, we quietly watched and hoped that you newly made humans would be allowed to evolve in a peaceful manner. We were prevented by the Oneness from interfering in the manipulation of your residual memories. Throughout time, many of the 'god' races were kind and ethical, but some of them were not and we were not allowed to step in and intercede on your behalf.

Each of us in Creation has a role to play and in your eyes it might seem that we are self-governing and all-powerful. To some extent that perception is accurate. We may have originated waves upon waves of life forms in many universes, yet, in the end, we too are answerable to the Oneness that is the source of all creation.

We simply waited and observed, as the Oneness instructed, to see if the human species could overcome the obstacles of imposed memory loss. We waited as the 'gods' came time after time to tinker with you humans and we did not interfere because the evolution of these so-called 'gods' was being evaluated too.

Those of us who watch and wait were quietly pleased to see that there were always rare exceptions to the memory disconnection that was done to you. You are sprinkled around the globe like a scattering of jewel-toned seeds in the wind. In every era of humankind, there have always been a handful of you that have remembered who you truly are and reconnected with those of us in all forms who reside on the other side of the veil.

The original source of your disconnection has been mentioned, but your own souls have made choices that perpetuated this disconnection as well. Many of you have chosen to return again and again to this damaged planet. When you are between lives and not in a state of incarnation, you are given choices for the location of your next life experience. But most of you have returned repeatedly to this world for a variety of reasons that have little to do with soul development.

Some of you eagerly came back to the 'Pleasure Planet' Earth—the planet of highs and lows of emotion that do not exist to such an extent elsewhere in this universe—because your souls had developed a type of addiction to these sensations. If you had never experienced this place firsthand, you may have been curious and perhaps you chose to find out for yourselves if it was as dense and 'sticky' with emotion as you had heard. But your soul path, both in and out of human incarnation, is yours to decide and free will allows you to choose when, where, or if you will incarnate on any world.

Know this as well—not every soul is warm and wise and all-knowing just because it reunites with the energy of the Oneness at the moment of death. Just as humans come in many shades and variations of energy and emotion, so do souls. There are those on this world who purport to be teachers of wisdom and they firmly state that the life-after-death world contains nothing but enlightened and unselfish beings since they are now basking in their reunion with the Oneness. That is not now and has never been a complete truth.

In a first-incarnation version, your soul may have arrived here at any time in the past or present simply to learn the lessons of Earth humanity. That is a simple process and it is ongoing. You will occasionally still meet someone who may tell you that they have always felt out of place, as if this is not where they were meant to be. Most of these people have experienced their prior lifetimes on other worlds and they are indeed correct when they state that Earth feels unfamiliar.

For some of you who have chosen to come here, the primary motivation is to be of service to this world. The generosity of spirit that is exhibited by those who come back to help is a tiny reflection of the 'best case' nature of your true selves when you are unhampered by the 'clothing' of human bodies.

Think back to what we have told you about the first humans, the ones who were able to communicate with us on the other side in every moment and at will. The mode of communication was tonal. Waves of tonal energy would vibrate silently from each and every being both human and non-human, incarnated or not, and amongst the plants, animals, and minerals.

The tones were almost musical in nature, unheard by the actual human ear, and they could only be 'heard' through the vibratory sensing mechanism of another equally open and aware being of any kind. Now what would happen if either the tones were altered or the sensing mechanism was shut off? There would be a disconnection from the energy of the Oneness and from those of us in other realms who had communicated freely with you in the past.

And what is the effect of the alteration of the tones? Instead of the pure and musical energy of your body-wrapped souls, in almost each and every case of human incarnation—EVERY body sings off key!

This has a much greater meaning than just the obvious separation from the nourishing contact with the life force on the other side of the veil of incarnation. It also means that you 'sing' to one another in a non-harmonious manner. Your souls are communicating with one another while you reside in Earth bodies in an out of tune mode—out of tune with your own sense of soul connection and out of tune with one another residing in the Earthly realm.

We make this next statement to emphasize how important it is to move beyond the desire for incarnation on this planet and to give your soul other options. With each and every incarnation on Earth, your tonal energy, your tonal vibration, your 'body song' is more and more skewed and out of tune.

So is it any wonder then that so few of you resonate strongly with a great many of the other humans that you meet? And is it any wonder that the ones you choose to partner with or befriend are frequently in a similar tonal range as yours? Flawed though it may be compared to what the early humans may have enjoyed, this tonal resonance is more important for long lasting human relationships than you could even imagine.

What human sciences call the chemical attraction of humans to one another is actually the chemicals in the body singing to one another in a resonance pattern that is agreeable to each of them. And your own body's chemicals may also have *no* desire to 'sing to' the chemicals of certain other humans.

This chemical song gives off an unheard-to-the-ear sound that vibrates pleasantly through the body and it also produces an unseen set of vibratory colours that weave you together tightly. This weaving is part of the survival mechanism of your species.

This is an important concept and we wish for people to understand the essential nature of harmonic vibration—both human and in physical objects. Your vibratory field can make the difference in the success of relationships, your ability to interact with animals, and even your ability to feel comfortable within a building such as your own home. If you are unable to maintain stable relationships, if you are unable to feel any kind of contact with the Oneness, if you feel more connected to animals or plants and minerals than you do to humans, you are simply feeling the effects of being 'off key' more than the average human does.

A partial solution is to try and retrain your body to 'sing' more clearly. We say with truth that it is only a partial solution since your entire planet is bombarded with non-stop sound and even in the places that you think are quiet spots in the country, invisible waves of electronic energy are constantly moving through your bodies and disrupting the molecules that comprise your body-suit.

We have spoken of those rare ones on your world who are able to access information from other realms—from places such as the depths of stillness where we reside. But even those blessed ones are challenged by sound. We have noted with pleasure that if they are effective meditators, they are able to 'switch off' their internal *and* external hearing and simply slide into the void. And in that place of no-place, the connections to the Oneness are more easily remembered and felt.

Just as the woman who is Deborah was able to register the sensation of us squeezing her small hand when she was a child, the sensation was communicated in a non-physical act of sending and her open young mind was able to 'feel' what we sent.

There is much to feel in that void. If you are able to reach that place where you have no expectation of what will happen, if you can leave the page unwritten upon, beings of wonder will step forth to share with you and yes, some of them will project into your mind a sensation of being gently and lovingly touched.

There is much wisdom that resides there when your heart quiets itself, your mind is still, time has no hold on you, and suddenly the only sound is that of the faintest echo of a wind that is not wind but is the sound of the stars. Within this place of no-place, your bodies and soul essences can begin to heal. And with each healing session, your body can once again begin to sing ON key.

Chapter Four

THE PARANORMAL
BECOMES NORMAL

When I first began to discuss these subjects with friends and acquaintances in the 1960s and 1970s, none of the people in my immediate circle had ever read any published material that referenced paranormal communication or psychic phenomena. In addition to the sudden groundswell of books written during that time for the mainstream audience, there were also more scholarly offerings written by researchers at forward thinking university programs in parapsychology such as the Rhine Research Institute at Duke University or by members of groups such as the Theosophical Society or the Society of Psychical Research.

I have chosen to share several personal episodes with the readers to explain the variety of phenomena that both a beginning or experienced seeker may encounter. As our collective increase in interest in all things paranormal surges, the types of events that I am about to describe, for good or not-good, are bound to escalate.

In a mirroring of the late-1800s through early 1900s interest in spiritualism, the pioneers in consciousness studies in the 1960s and 1970s began the dialogue once again. Primarily centred on the West Coast and East Coast of the USA, those of us growing up in the middle parts of the country such as my own childhood home in Louisville, Kentucky had to look long and hard for even the few books on those topics that were offered in our local libraries—books written by authors such as Raymond Moody and Ruth Montgomery or based on the work of Edgar Cayce.

Some of the questions posed by the 20th-century seekers were age-old but still quite valid. Why are we here and what is our purpose? Is this the only life we ever live? What do other cultures believe about incarnation and spiritual enlightenment? Does life exist on other planets and why are UFOs visiting Earth? What happened to the amazing technology from previous civilisations and why did those people die off or simply disappear?

From the 1980s onward there was an huge upsurge in the next wave of curiosity about all things alternative with people jumping on the New Age bandwagon and a sudden explosion of interest in the many ways to find more meaning in life than what we could see, hear, and touch in our day to day lives. Those seekers could feel that change was imminent even if the change that they sensed was several decades away from its actual time of appearance. Workshops were available in almost every metaphysical or new age bookstore and some of those topics were how to connect with your spirit guides, how to contact angels, opening your chakras, communication with the dead, tarot reading for future predictions, past life regression, and channelling.

The short definition of channelling means receiving information from sources outside the realms of normal three-dimensional life. Because this is a subject close to my heart based on my own contact with not-of-this-world beings from childhood onward, I have chosen to attend both public and private sessions in many places around the world. It has been both interesting and occasionally saddening to hear the followers of each channeller proclaim that they were the very best, the most reliable, the most accurate, and that the information was astonishing. Unfortunately, that was rarely the case.

During one four-year period when I was living in Florida, my then husband and I attended several evening sessions at different bookstores in St. Augustine and Jacksonville Beach in the late 1980s and very early 1990s with distinctly mixed results. Some of the presenters were brilliant and authentic and several of them were outright fakes. But I always noted that the fakes had just as large a following as the ones who were stunningly truthful.

You may ask how I determined who was false and who was not. Many people would call it a 'gut instinct'—but in my own case I experience a range of tones in my body that resonate in my head and various tones tell if what I am hearing or seeing is truth or fiction.

There was one older woman who was one of the regular presenters in St. Augustine and she was one of the few really reliable mediums that we ever saw during this period. I will not give her name since she is deceased now and I don't have the permission of her family to do so.

Sometimes during her sessions at the bookstore, her guide, a pickpocket who had lived in London in the early 1800s, would appear and talk to us. But she always made it clear that this was not higher soul-level knowledge but spirit knowledge from the other side—nothing more. She was also a classically trained spiritualist medium who was able to contact relatives who had passed over and would pass on messages from them.

My husband and I were sitting in the audience one night when I actually should have been home in bed—but I had made the reservations long before I knew that I would be having surgery that week and I was reluctant to miss out on the evening. It was only the second time that we had seen her in the last year and we were quite happy to just sit and listen and we didn't ask for any communication or clarification for ourselves.

We sat down and after a brief introduction, the woman led us in a group meditation so that we could all be in a peaceful frame of mind as we listened. After she had finished with the meditation session, she began talking to us about general things and suddenly she stopped, became silent for a moment as she scanned the audience, and then turned to point right at me and ask, "What's wrong with you? You have some kind of damage to your body and you are leaking light energy out of your aura."

I had not spoken to anyone as we arrived that evening and no one at the book store knew that I had just gotten out of the hospital the day before.

She waited for me to answer, but when I hesitated to say anything in front of a group of strangers, she said, "It's some kind of surgery isn't it? You've been cut open and that has left cuts in your auric field."

Without waiting for me to answer, she looked at my husband who was quietly nodding yes and she came down from the raised platform and over to me, saying to the rest of the audience, "Just be patient while I do this. It will take a minute or two."

She closed her eyes very briefly and then began to swoosh her hands in the air up and down the sides of my body as if she was smoothing down some invisible ragged edges. After she finished, she held my hands for a minute since I had begun to silently cry. She got down close to my face and said that it was perfectly normal to be traumatized on all kinds of levels after surgery and I just nodded yes, and managed to gasp out, "I know" and a quick thank you as huge tears flowed down my face.

She patted me on the knee, pulled her nearing-70-year-old body into an upright position, asked the bookshop owner to bring me a cup of tea, and she went straight back to the subjects that she had begun discussing previously.

At the end of the evening, she left quickly. It was her usual practice and she discouraged those who lingered afterward from talking-it-to-death about the subjects that had been covered during her sessions. She was surrounded by people trying to get her attention as she pressed through the crowd and I never even got close enough to her to say another thank you.

I was in that bookshop about six months later and heard that she had moved up north to be closer to her married children and grandchildren and died shortly afterwards. I may never have gotten to speak to her directly again, but the authenticity of her words and actions still resonates in my heart.

By 1994, I was on my own again, living and travelling in Britain as I worked on my Master's degree. There were New Age shops in abundance, all overflowing with offerings of workshops of every kind, and these were well attended in every city and village around Britain. Curiosity poked me in the back some days and I attended a few workshops and reading sessions in England that were just as revealing about the nature of truth and fraud walking hand in hand as those earlier sessions in the USA or the ones to come in Australia.

There was a very popular New Age centre in the theatre district of London and I should have listened to my inner instincts which told me that the atmosphere in the place was 'off' somehow. But I was in the midst of some personal crisis or the other as I juggled graduate school, a divorce, and financial questions and I felt the need to consult an outside source. It was to be one of the last times I ever looked outside of myself for guidance.

In these litigious times, I feel that I should not mention the name of the shop. But I walked in there with an open heart and an open mind during a mid-week lull when they were not filled with the usual weekend throng of browsers and I made an appointment for a reading that day. What a huge disappointment it turned out to be and I left there feeling truly resentful about the money I had spent. Later, many weeks later to be truthful, I realised that it had been a valuable lesson.

The man sat in his chair with a sort of velvet beret perched atop his head and he plainly needed a bath and a liberal dose of deodorant. This was the person that the counter clerk had said was "so good that he was scary?" As I waited patiently, he sipped his tea and laid out the cards on the table. Then he took both of my hands, scrutinized the lines on them and made some funny sounds as if he was pondering how to present the information.

Suddenly he cleared his throat and launched into his interpretation of my reading. Either I was a very good actress that day or he was completely oblivious since he never seemed to notice how dreadfully wrong he was on every count. I simply sat passively and said "Oh, I see" as I nodded occasionally.

He predicted that a relative would die and leave me a substantial fortune. This event was supposed to transpire within a twelve month period, but here we are, over fifteen years later, and no such inheritance has ever arrived.

Next he 'saw' me marrying an extremely wealthy man that I met in France within six months and living in a grand house in the country. Well, I did marry a man that I met overseas, but he was a lovely Australian fellow that I met in London and we've never, ever had a grand house in the country or been awash with cash.

After sipping his tea and staring silently at the cards for awhile, he next pronounced that within a few years I would be struggling with a serious depression that would leave me bedridden as I attempted to decide between my career as an executive and my life with this man in France. I have never aspired to be an executive and I find that sort of life admirable for other people, but not the least bit desirable for myself. And we already know that there was never to be any man in France.

Finally he saw me back in the USA for awhile, embroiled in a dramatic family argument over my decision to throw aside my career and follow my Frenchman off to the countryside. I can assure you that there was never any family argument, there was never a French husband, and my family thought it was rather wonderful that I got to travel around the world and live in other cultures and countries.

So, the verdict? Wrong, wrong, wrong! Everything he told me was wrong! But I had paid for the reading at the beginning and it was too late for a refund. When he asked me how I felt about all of it though, I did tell him that I thought he was rather drastically off the mark and he countered that I was "being negative" and that I needed to realise that these things hadn't unfolded yet. So according to the foul-smelling man in the velvet beret, I needed to be patient and just allow it all to happen.

When the girl at the counter asked me how it went as I was exiting the shop, I told her honestly that it was the worst reading that I'd ever had and that I felt that the man was an utter fraud. She looked quite shocked. But that reading was not the last episode of New Age fraud that I was to witness.

On another occasion in Brisbane, Australia in 1996, I watched a woman give the most astonishing performance as a supposed channeller. She could have been an actress in the local amateur drama society for all of the reality or truthfulness that was portrayed that evening.

The friend who took us to this session had been attending this woman's meetings for several years and he made a point of telling her when he introduced us that I had just finished doing my Master's thesis on Spiritual and Paranormal Studies and was soon to begin a Ph.D. on a similar topic. Her face betrayed her as she looked moderately panicked for a moment, but then she forged ahead and asked everyone to find a seat and get settled.

Demanding in a firm voice that the lights be dimmed, she closed her eyes and sat making funny sounds as she trembled all over rather violently, and then her 'entity' took over. The first thing that I noticed was that her accent kept changing dramatically and that the voice of 'the entity' sounded Scandinavian, then Irish, then British, and finally quite Australian. The 'entity' claimed to be one of many advanced space aliens from another planet who were here to save us humans from ourselves.

The pronouncements that followed left me alternating between muted giggling and quiet fury as she told her band of faithful followers to not read any books other than those she wrote so that it wouldn't "muddle their minds." Then she proceeded to paraphrase from nearly every New Age book that had been published ten to fifteen years earlier in the United States.

As she sat there solemnly intoning a bit of this book and a bit of that and claiming that it was all her own original information from the 'entity,' I became more and more stunned when I looked at the enraptured faces of her innocent victims. Most of these people visited her twice a week and paid $50 each session for the privilege of, unbeknownst to them, receiving recycled material from other sources. I was simply astonished at the gullibility factor on display by that point.

Then she capped it off by telling them that for the next week they were to only eat orange foods. I wanted to shriek aloud, "Are you people crazy to listen to this?"—but I kept still as the 'entity' explained that the current earthly vibrations needed a supplement of orange hues to balance their unstable auras.

The 'entity' then announced that it was departing, and we had another episode of violent shaking and moaning followed by a weak voice asking that the lights be brought up gradually.

As she opened her eyes, she looked straight at me. She wanted to see if I had determined what she was doing. And I let her know with a smirk and a nod that I had nailed it straight away.

Her face was more than a little bit panicked as I walked up to her while the devoted band swirled around her like bees, gasping at the brilliance of her session that night. My friend who had brought me to the session had not asked her for permission beforehand and when we discussed it in the car on the ride home, he realised that she would have probably said no.

Instead of being rude, I walked up to her, hugged her tersely, and said, "Interesting evening!" And out the door we walked. I didn't even contemplate a confrontation over her lack of truthfulness in front of her band of followers. It was her 'home turf' and it would have been churlish of me to stand there and point a finger at her and say, "What a fake!" It would also have served no purpose since those gullible folks would have raced across the room to defend her authenticity.

As our friend drove us home that night, I asked him how much money he had spent on that charlatan over the last few years and he stammered a bit and never really answered the question. He sheepishly said that he had harboured doubts for a while, but no one else seemed any better than she was and he was so longing to find something authentic to connect with each week that he was willing to suspend his disbelief and just keep paying her.

I had to keep myself in check just then as I wanted to say something edgy to this man who should have known better but who clearly didn't. What came out of my mouth was actually a moderate response as I told our friend that maybe it was a step on the path to being a spiritual seeker that all of the followers of this charlatan needed to take. Perhaps, for whatever reason that I could not imagine, they needed the experience of being lied to and cheated financially so that they would recognise those kinds of frauds in the future.

In direct contrast to that distinctly dodgy woman was the spiritualist medium that a dear friend in Brisbane introduced me to the following year. This lovely woman was in her 80s and had been trained as a classical medium during her early adulthood in Wales. She made me a cup of tea and we sat at her kitchen table, chatting a bit about the friends that we had in common. After about a half an hour, she picked up a deck of plain playing cards and asked me to hold them for a few minutes, shuffle them, and then hand them back to her. She then laid the cards on the table and, staring straight down at the cards, she began to discuss various aspects of things that she saw coming into my future.

Suddenly she looked up and said that the spirits of several people were standing all around me, just behind my shoulders. Within minutes, a stream of information was coming from her mouth, information that only I could have known about various relatives or past events in our family history. I must also mention that when we had our initial chat over that cup of tea, no mention was ever made of my family or my past. We simply talked about the people that we both knew in common.

Although the information that she gave me that day was not particularly earth shattering in its importance, I was deeply touched by the messages that she gave me from departed relatives. Many of these messages were actually quite humourous, referenced episodes in my childhood, and the dear little woman had no way of knowing why I was chuckling so hard until I explained afterward. It was quite an interesting afternoon and I can unreservedly state that she was completely genuine.

Each of the episodes above happened over a decade ago, and there are similar versions of the same things happening now. Just as I found the wonderfully authentic psychic channeller in St. Augustine and the sweet little spiritualist medium in Brisbane, you too will encounter readers who are truthful and gifted.

But as a gentle warning, please maintain a stance of alertness to the knowledge that there are always those who claim to be wise and knowing who are plainly not. If the tiniest bit of doubt flickers across your consciousness when you are about to engage with someone or something new in this realm, pay attention to those feelings and honour that early warning. And for heaven's sake, don't be swayed by the opinions of well-meaning friends who pressure you by telling you that this person or thing is *the* must-have contact. Your own inner guidance is your most reliable resource!

Changing Perceptions

Although we have come a long way in the last twenty years toward a more open-minded attitude to alternative concepts, I still notice that when or if metaphysical subjects are covered in mainstream media reports such as a segment on the morning or evening news, they are glossed over with a kind of smirking tongue-in-cheek approach meant to plainly convey to the bulk of the viewers that the television station certainly doesn't take such things seriously. I have accidentally tuned in to an hour of the morning news here in Australia on at least three occasions in the last year during an interview with a psychic or a segment on UFO sightings around the world. In each instance, the female half of the morning team was polite and interested in what was being said whilst the male half of the on-air partnership practically dripped with sarcasm.

If this type of rude and dismissive attitude is still being absorbed by the viewers around the country, is it any wonder that so many believers in alternative theories choose to keep those beliefs firmly to themselves? These attitudes are not unique to Australia. As I am writing this book at the end of 2009, I unfortunately still encounter people in my day-to-day life who want to discuss what they feel and sense, but they dare not upset their family or spouses, so they stay achingly silent.

There has been, however, an interesting and gratifying shift in the television and movie industry where metaphysical concepts are concerned during the past decade. The number of shows devoted to these topics grows each year and as I type this, the North American or British produced television shows *Medium, Fringe, Supernatural, Heroes, Ghost Whisperer, Eureka, The Dresden Files, Torchwood, Afterlife, Stargate Universe,* and the many variations of the *Star Trek* franchise are amongst the top-rated television series world wide. Sometimes dark and mysterious, sometimes presented in a semi-comedic vein, several of the shows named above, as well as others that have not yet arrived in Australia, address variables in the current state of human physiology and mental or psychic abilities and the new frontiers ahead.

I wrote about the possibility of this type of 'emerging human' consciousness in an unpublished book written in 1994 as my Master of Arts thesis, so it is gratifying to see this subject being examined in a popular media format that brings it to the attention of a larger group of people.

The films that are emerging from Hollywood and Europe with a metaphysical or predictive overtone are far too numerous to mention at this point, but I will touch on it lightly.

The Matrix (1999–2003) trilogy of movies revealed some revolutionary ideas about the interconnectedness of all life, the illusion of human form as the 'vessel' for the soul or consciousness, the manipulation of the human species by 'creator gods', and the multiple 'cycles' of humans on earth whilst the 'creator gods' refined their end product. These were ideas which may have been rejected as too bizarre to be produced by mainstream movie studios a mere few years earlier. But think of what the filmmakers were trying to portray in light of the emerging information from the world's physicists about the nature of time, space, and reality. The public embraced these films wholeheartedly and clamoured for more.

The Butterfly Effect (2004) explores the possible paradoxes that would occur if you could change the events in the past. Both *The Fountain*, and *Deja Vu* (both released in 2006) are concerned with the same theme. What few realise is that this manipulation of time actually exists in the real world and has been enacted upon humankind repeatedly as a means of keeping us asleep and unaware. In some cases the time-twisters are from sources outside of our current world, but in almost as many cases the Puppet Masters that run the global control machine have learned from their out-of-this-time brothers and they now manipulate the facts and reality to suit their skewed purpose.

The wonderfully spooky film *The Mothman Prophecies* (2002) is based on a true series of incidents that took place in West Virginia. The nature of alternative time-space is at the very crux of this film since the creature plainly does not dwell within our own time and space and simply emerges through some opening between worlds to briefly interact with humans. That is exactly what *does* occur in many of the sightings of animals, events, or beings that do not belong in our world. It is a bleedthrough from another reality and this reality-intrusion includes creatures such as the Loch Ness 'monster' and many of the sightings of UFOs.

I was fortunate to meet the creator of *Star Trek,* Gene Roddenberry, when he came to speak at the University of Kentucky in the early 1980s while I was a student there. I was actually quite surprised to see that there was a relatively small turnout for that midweek evening discussion, but I surmised that it was because the original television series had been off the air for over a decade and *Star Trek: The Next Generation* was yet to arrive on our television screens.

Roddenberry gave a brief talk lasting less than an hour where he related funny stories about how difficult it had been to sell the television networks on the feasibility of a series that was set in outer space. What finally brought them around and allowed him to secure the money needed to film the pilot episode was his pitch that *Star Trek* would be just like their most popular show, *Wagon Train,* only instead of a western with covered wagons travelling across the American frontier having weekly adventures, it would be a spaceship exploring "space: the final frontier" with a cast of characters that the audience would soon grow to love.

He groaned and grinned as he explained that this was his way of getting a foot in the door for what he really wanted to do—discuss social issues that ranged from racial or ethnic bigotry to the unequal treatment of women. If Roddenberry had ever told those network executives the real truth, there never would have been a pilot episode, much less a series that turned out to be a cult classic.

One thing stuck in my mind as he spoke. He said that a great many people looked at the show as entertainment only and considered it to be a form of animated comic book. But apparently not all of the more executive members of the military thought so. He explained that he had been visited by members of the U.S. Air Force during the second year of the series and they asked him some rather pointed questions about whether he had been in contact with any members of the military or the space program. Some of the men in the corridors of power had sent these officers to find out if he was creating his stories after hearing first hand about some of the ongoing research that may or may not have been under way in top secret laboratories. And they were especially interested in his portrayal of the transporter. Roddenberry laughed as he told this episode because he said he realised just how close he was to real-world potentials and that made him quite amused to be making the military a bit uncomfortable.

A mere handful of people stayed behind after the talk to ask any questions and I was one of the five people who, along with Roddenberry, moved into an empty classroom and sat chatting for awhile. I was amused to see that I was the only woman who had any questions to ask and I quietly waited as 'the boys' all asked their questions about potential future series and the technology on the show. Then they said goodnight and drifted out of the room—all except one of them who hovered in the doorway and listened as I asked whether the inspiration for the scenes of the future came totally from his imagination, or were they also a result of dreams or visions. The silence in the room was acute and momentarily awkward. Then Roddenberry shifted in his seat, stood up and walked two steps toward me, and said,

"You know things, don't you?" And with that he shook my hand, smiled broadly, and walked out of the room.

To continue on the outer space theme and very briefly touch on the UFO phenomenon, it is my strong belief (and one which the Dreamkeeper discussed with me decades ago) that there are multiple sources for the sightings of what we call UFOs. Some of them are from other time periods both past and forward and they come through an opening into our time for a quick perusal of our current state of evolution or devolution. Others are beings who have always co-existed with us in a case of hiding in plain sight as demonstrated in the film, *The Abyss*. Finally, some of the off-world UFOs are very likely to be similar to the ones portrayed in *Close Encounters Of The Third Kind*. In all three cases, the major governments of the world have always known who they were and where they came from, so their continued pattern of denial is ludicrous.

The Dreamkeeper whispers to me some days and on other ones she positively shouts at me. "Heads up! You are being given advance warning of what the scientists and world leaders already know is on the way. The weather will change and grow more deadly, the face of the planet will change and grow less hospitable, mass extinctions will unfold amongst many species of plants and animals, the nature of Earth's life amongst the stars will change, and humankind is about to take a massive leap forward in understanding their true place within the overall scheme of things."

We are moving, like it or not, into a state of evolution that few could have imagined a mere few years ago. And the filmmakers and writers of the world are broadcasting that message of unmistakable, unavoidable, impending change ahead of its arrival. There is a conscious plan that has been underway for the last few decades and that plan is to educate the masses through popular media in a way that makes the pending changes easily understandable to all no matter what level of education an individual may possess. In some cases the message is delivered in such an *un*-subtle way as to be cartoonish, but these message-producers certainly do understand the short attention span of their target market.

Beyond the conditioning-for-change propaganda being distributed on film, why are both the paranormal and visions of the future now of such interest to the everyday reader or viewer? Why has this particular set of topics mushroomed on our television and film screens and why is the New Age or metaphysical area of your local bookstore one of the fastest growing areas?

In spite of the constant dumbing down of education for the masses and the blatant talking down to us that is done by the media in all forms, many of us, young and old alike, have had a sensation that this interest in the spiritual (not religious) and otherworldly has been long overdue. Perhaps we felt a deep longing for the other people around us to wake up to what we already knew within our hearts. I honestly could never have anticipated this blossoming interest in all of these topics a mere decade ago and I am grateful to see it finally unfolding. But the unfolding carries a sense of responsibility and we must each strive to be the best version of ourselves as we move forward into this exciting and slightly daunting new energy.

If the impending energy changes that we are on the cusp of find us with the sci-fi like abilities to read minds and know the truth of things instantly, it will prove to be a great challenge to the world leaders who have lied to their populations in order to maintain control by any means necessary. If we are able to see through that veil of lies, what does that portend for the stability of societies? How do we balance the need to redress the wrongs that have been done with the need to maintain a sense of order? An excess of action such as rioting or revolution, without prior consideration for the long term outcome, could prove to be just as dangerous as living in a permanent state of childish acceptance of anything that 'the leaders' say we must believe and do. We must strive for balance in all action and thought.

And if, as I believe, such populist offerings as *What The Bleep Do We Know* and *The Secret* are the baby-food introduction to our soon-to-arrive ability to manifest both things and actions in an instant, we must all learn to carefully consider each and every thought or word before we fling them out of our minds or mouths and into the world as a real item or event. We are going to need to maintain a purity of intent at all times to keep both ourselves and the world safe!

Our quest for more, for the secrets of time and space and our place in it, has proven to be infectious and now a new generation or two of spiritual and psychic explorers has arrived, some of whom may be our own children and grandchildren. There seems to be a wonderful overlap of age groups where the psychic and paranormal are concerned. with the open hearts and minds of several generations embracing the films and television series that I mentioned in previous paragraphs.

As a mirror of our present day and our on-the-doorstep times, the film, television, and gaming industries along with many writers are certainly giving us a lot to digest! And there will be many more of these 'training experiences' portrayed in our media in the coming years.

Chapter Five
ALTERNATIVE METHODS

There is a worrying upsurge in the way all things psychic and paranormal, in conjunction with various forms of experimental practice, have been taken up by the military and government agencies. But this is not a new occurrence and it has been going on for quite a few decades with deeper roots in our contemporary past than most people can imagine. Covert groups employed by various world governments have utilised paranormal methodology to either spy on other nations or specific individuals and have used these methods as a way of influencing behaviour or perception for a long time.

In an interesting set of 'revelations' during the last several years, it has become common knowledge that the United States government in particular, and many other governments in a spirit of competitiveness, have hosted extensive programs in what is now called Remote Viewing. The Federation of American Scientists has an entire page describing the activities of remote viewing programs such as Star Gate.[3]

These programs are purported to have only been active from the 1960s through 1990s and have now supposedly been disbanded altogether. Somehow, I rather doubt that! This was too valuable a method to have simply been abandoned after so many decades and I now know that remote viewing is accompanied by machine-based enhancements that 'learn' through each remote viewing episode. I will discuss that later in this chapter.

Remote viewing (RV) is similar to out-of-body travels in that it involves the ability to see and perceive places, objects, and people that are not within the physical viewing area of the person. Several variations on this type of psychic viewing were utilised by various world governments in attempts to find ways to not only spy on one another, but also to uncover the nature of life on other planets.

This well-funded research was a contemporary twist on an age old pursuit for knowledge of the unknown. Psychic visionaries have used a variety of means such as scrying (a form of divination that involves gazing into a bowl of still water or a crystal ball to obtain otherworldly visions), shamanic quests via hallucinogenic substances, mystical encounters whilst in prayer or trance, and other types of altered-state experiences to access the present or future.

Within the last few years, written accounts have emerged, some published by eminent scientists, that point to some rather amazing success with some of the recent versions of this spying-from-a-distance. As a result of the supposed dismantling of the officially sanctioned government programs, many of the 'first generation' remote viewers and instructors have gone on to write books on the subject for general readership and sponsor workshops where they train ordinary people in these RV techniques.

Beyond these populist offerings, there is still valid scientific research being conducted in research centres around the world and some of this cutting edge work indicates a distinct overlap between the remote viewers and the realm of quantum physics. I highly approve of this aspect of remote viewing and it is a subject matter of considerable interest to both my husband and myself. As part of the research for my next book, we plan to delve into this more thoroughly.

One example of this scholarly approach is discussed in the 2005 book *Remote Viewing: The Science and Theory of Nonphysical Perception* by Courtney Brown, Ph.D. This book is aimed at both the lay reader and those with a rigorous science background.

I can also highly recommend Russell Targ's *Limitless Mind*. One of the co-founders in 1972 of the Stanford Research Institute program to investigate psychic phenomena, Targ has since gone on to write several books and conduct teaching seminars in remote viewing and healing at a distance.

Targ takes a step-by-step approach in his description of the many stages that psi research has taken along the path to remote viewing. His method of relating the ups and downs along the way is quite humorous and I would think that one of his workshops would be both informative and fun.

A direct contrast to the serious intent of the above discussed research can be seen at several websites, aimed at the general public, where they plainly state on the opening page that learning RV can allow you to find out anything about anyone no matter where they are in the world.

Why would an ordinary man or woman need to learn this method that was formerly the purview of the military? I can understand the use of these techniques in criminal investigation, quantum physics, or even in the ongoing research that is being conducted in afterlife studies, but why are these workshops so heavily marketed to people who are not 'in the field' of scientific, psychic, or spiritual research?

The human greed factor and voyeuristic impulses are apparently being catered to when the advertising for these sites claim that you can win a fortune at the race track or casino, peek at your neighbours to see what they are doing, and spy on your business competition to get one up on them. It unfortunately sounds as if the RV trainers on these sites are aiming their focus at the lowest common denominator of student—not those with lofty intentions.

To shift gears a bit, information is now being introduced to the public that allows them to know that the ever-evolving neural technology field has found a way to link human brain activities with technological hardware. I find these types of press releases a bit disingenuous since the research has plainly been in the works for decades prior to this 'amazing new technology' publicity blitz.

In a June 2009 episode of *60 Minutes* on CBS television in the USA, reporters interviewed scientists who are doing groundbreaking research with MRI scans that can 'read' your thoughts to reveal what you are looking at and even tell where you have been.

How Technology May Soon "Read" Your Mind

"I always tell my students that there is no science fiction anymore. All the science fiction I read in high school, we're doing," Paul Root Wolpe, director of the Center for Ethics at Emory University in Atlanta, told Stahl.[4]

One of the many reasons that I am highly skeptical of the 'newness' of this particular technology is due to those life-long visions that I have received. Within the past year I was conversing online with a cluster of friends and we were discussing the emerging technology. I was noting my concern with the overlap into psychology-based consciousness studies and I mentioned that the things that we were reading in the daily newspaper were just the tip of the iceberg of the devices that had already been invented and which were being used every day by various agencies around the world.

Suddenly I had a strong visual flash in my head of an object that was not much larger than a mobile phone. Agents working for some government's spy agency were sitting in a plain, dark vehicle and then they exited to walk amongst a crowd of people in an urban park during lunch hour. The city had the 'feel' of a large metropolis in the USA due to the style of buildings, the type of clothing worn, and the general appearance of the people.

I heard no voices and it was a totally silent vision, but the agents exiting the car and mingling amongst the people began to engage in a type of field research. Holding those innocuous looking phone-like devices, they circulated through the crowds, occasionally stopping to pretend to make a call and subtly aim them at pairs or groups of people who were talking. And according to the readings on the fake mobile phones, the agents could determine who was telling the truth as they spoke and who was not. The energy signatures of the individuals who were targeted were giving off readings much like a lie-detector would. But in this case, there was no direct contact with the person that was being read. It was all being conducted surreptitiously and remotely.

Reprogramming Methodology

There is no doubt in my own mind that the so-called dismantling of the psychic spying programs by the various military intelligence agencies is a complete fabrication. I believe that they are ongoing today under new names and with new high-tech methodology like the ones described in the articles above. But the technological 'toys' are apparently not enough and these agencies continue to refine their use of pharmacology as a means of delving into the thoughts of others.

Recently there have been mentions in several scientific journals of a new wonder drug that is designed to erase painful memories. This drug is purported to be aimed at alleviating the anxiety that accompanies Post Traumatic Stress Disorder, but it doesn't take a huge leap of imagination to realise that it could also be used to alter the memories of people who were considered 'problematic' by any government or intelligence agency.

On the 26th of November 2006, CBS News in the USA did a broadcast report on this very topic. The article mentioned that although it gave great relief to some people, some of the subjects were plainly disturbed about the feelings of intrusion into their thought processes.

One of the women subjects stated, *"It's like they went in and altered my mind." "This study has taken away a part of me that's been in me for so long, and that I find very weird."*

The ethical dilemma of memory removal or alteration has been repeatedly examined in literature and film over the last several decades and once again, I believe that those portrayals on film are an intentional means of conditioning the public to methods readily available in the intelligence communities. Both versions of the film *The Manchurian Candidate*, the first in 1962 and the second in 2004, were concerned with implanting false memories which would trigger later action. Other films that focused on the issue of memory or memory alteration are *Eternal Sunshine of the Spotless Mind*, *Memento*, and *Dark City*.

A book which examines the concepts of an artificially created individual utopia that is achievable through memory alteration and which is frequently cited in both philosophy and psychology classes is *Anarchy, State, and Utopia* by Robert Nozick. In it he writes of the possibility of an extraordinary machine that can give you any experience that you wish. However, whilst that so-called experience is happening, you are actually lying in a state of unconsciousness and are hooked up to a machine that produces this faux world that you are walking around in. It would seem that Nozick was rather prescient when he wrote that book in 1977.

How passive would you be though if you knew that 'subcontractors' working for a government agency have the ability to reprogram your brain and its memories through auditory, visual, and altered state "psychological correction'. Information can now be swiftly extracted from the subject's consciousness without the person even knowing that they have revealed anything. Visual effects are so subtly layered into the daily background that the subject never sees them and the background 'hum' of their daily lives is overlaid with subliminal background sounds or phrases.

Intelligence agencies routinely utilise specially-adapted yet ordinary-looking computer monitors that place you into an altered state while you sit there typing the answers to their questions or being programmed by the images and phrases which flash in the background as you type. The days of injecting so called 'truth serums' into a helpless victim and then waiting for them to spill their secrets is long gone.

Today's methodology is a continuation of the World War II and post-war research done by dubious pioneers such as

Donald Ewen Cameron. This one man worked for the OSS during the war and then for both British Intelligence and the CIA after WWII. His cold-blooded techniques were the basis of some of the real method of *Manchurian Candidate* style memory removal and subsequent repatterning of the psyche of a subject.[5]

I found much of this information to be both fascinating and repugnant at the same time. Given that my research involved transcripts from the the late 1930s through the early 1950s, imagine what can be done in our own time with the chemical and technological assistance available to the intelligence agencies. It is chilling to even contemplate that.

Travelling Through Time and Space

Five years ago an article in *USA Today* noted that the United States military was requesting funding for experimentation on a psychic teleportation device. How much further along than this do you suppose that the military already was back then before they decided to 'reveal' this information to the world.

Air Force report calls for $7.5M to study psychic teleportation

Star Trek fans may be happy to hear that the Air Force has paid to study psychic teleportation. But scientists aren't so thrilled. The Air Force Research Lab's August "Teleportation Physics Report," posted earlier this week on the Federation of American Scientists (FAS) Web site, struck a raw nerve with physicists and critics of wasteful military spending. In the report, author Eric Davis says psychic teleportation, moving yourself from location to location through mind powers, is "quite real and can be controlled. [6]

Ah, but is this 'new' teleportation really anything new at all? I believe not!

Within the last few years, and even as recently as the last few weeks, I have had a significant number of either intense dreams or waking visions on variations of this very topic. Keep in mind that until the military or world governments deign to 'reveal' this technology to the public in their little media blurbs, I have absolutely no way of proving to sceptics that my visions are accurate. However, given my success rate over the last many decades, I would be willing to bet that I am either spot on or eerily close to the truth in what I am seeing!

Out-of-Body Travels

The Egyptian, Chinese, and Hindu cultures are but three of the civilisations past and present that believed in subtle or ethereal out-of-body travels so this is not a new concept by any means. Throughout various cultures worldwide, the written records of events such as out-of-body travel were primarily of interest to the followers of each particular spiritual tradition. During the medieval Christian period, mystics spoke of departing from their body and flying outward to commune with Jesus or the angels. And in the mid-1700s, Swedish mystic and philosopher Emanuel Swedenborg wrote of his many out of body experiences. His writings strongly influenced many spiritually inclined artists, writers, and scientists for the next two hundred years including William Butler Yeats, William Blake, Carl Jung, and Elizabeth Barrett Browning.

An upsurge in interest in the early twentieth century began a more detailed chronicling of these types of experiences in books that were easily understandable by the general reading public. *The Projection of The Astral Body*, published in 1929 by American authors Sylvan Muldoon and Hereward Carrington, thoroughly documented the astral projections of Muldoon and gave instructions to the reader regarding how to accomplish this feat.

Hugh Callaway, a pioneering British researcher who had his first astral travel session in 1902 and who wrote under the pseudonym Oliver Fox, published a landmark book on the subject in 1938 entitled *Astral Projection*.

In my visions I saw quite a few small groups sprinkled around Europe, Britain, and the USA, sometimes in 1920s clothing, sometimes in 1930s attire and these groups often met in the homes of fellow spiritual and psychic investigators. At other times I saw them gathered in a place that looked like a church hall and those gatherings felt more 'lively' and full of activity compared to the more quiet research I saw within the private homes. I had a strong sense that these people would not have considered it at all unusual to be asked to have a look around during those travels and to report back to the group about what they saw.

The World War II Viewers

She read the piece of paper carefully and then handed it back to the man in the navy blue uniform who was standing in front of her. He nodded briskly and said, "Ready then?" Her salt and pepper curls bobbed up and down as she nodded her head in the affirmative and settled deeply into the chair. Her feet were elevated on a footstool and the temperature was cozy in this book-lined and wood-paneled library. The uniformed man left the room, clos-

ing the door quietly behind him, She closed her eyes and prepared to go travelling.

Today's destination was deep behind the German lines and she was planning to walk around invisibly in a General's office and then come back to tell her uniformed superiors about the maps and paperwork and plans she had secured within that near-photographic memory of hers. This unassuming middle-aged woman had succeeded so many times on her previous 'sleep travels" that she had no doubts about her ability to do this mission. And so she slept, knowing that within minutes she would be silently gliding through the hallways of the German High Command.

The vision that I have related above was received in the middle of 2009. Having just finished my lunch, I was taking a short break from working on this manuscript and as I began reading a travel book on architectural sites in Italy, I fell asleep. I had recently begun to read books on any subject *other* than psychic sensing to give myself a bit of 'mental vacation', so I was quite surprised by what happened next.

Immediately upon awakening, I scrambled for my laptop which was on the table next to me and words began to pour out of my fingers and onto the screen. The vision of the British woman who invisibly walked the halls of the German High Command came through quite clearly even if was a brief little 'mind movie' compared to some that I have had. And it certainly wasn't influenced by my pre-nap reading!

Going backward in time to when I first began to gather material for this book, about five years ago I had a series of *strong* dreams and then a waking vision regarding RV. In it, there were trained people during WWII who were doing this work watching the Germans, but the Germans were watching them right back! At that time in 2004, I said to my husband Mark that it would make a great movie—much like the movie *Enigma* with Kate Winslet—since I 'saw' the psychic researchers being plucked from the various branches of the British, American, Canadian, and Australian military. Members of a well-established psychical research group in Great Britain were partly responsible for the initial training and they worked right alongside the military members as civilian staff. But there were other people in charge of the training who 'felt' like either medical or laboratory-science personnel.

In my visions, I saw these people sequestered in both a large and semi-crumbling country manor which had been appropriated by the military for their use during the war and within two converted houses right in the heart of London and within central Edinburgh. The intelligence community had actually requested the services of these viewers and were open-minded about the results.

Back when I had the original set of visions and dreams, I was quite frustrated that I could never find any references to WWII era psychic spying in either books in print or through website searches. And of course a primary stumbling block in our present-day world is that almost all of those people would be dead by now and no longer available to share their stories. I also knew that it could very well be that the Ministry of Defense in Britain still considers this work to be highly secretive and they are reluctant to allow the general public to know that they used psychics to help win the war.

A tiny few pieces of information have now 'leaked out' for public consumption courtesy of books written in the years following my first set of visions on this topic. I was quite excited when I stumbled across these tantalising snippets after being stymied in my previous efforts to find even one reference to organised and officially sanctioned 1930s and 1940s psychic spying.

In once instance that I recently uncovered, Winston Churchill very quietly awarded a Jamaican man with a medal after the war for his psychic input that was essential to the war effort. An April 2009 press release from Reuters states, *"British Jamaican Jewish seer, kabalist and African-American World War II hero, Dr. Ernesto Moshe Montgomery, whose predictions and prophecies as a member of the British Intelligence service MI-5 during World War II contributed to the Allied Victory over Nazi Germany, is having his story published by Doubleday & Co. in a book titled* Psychic Spy: The Story of an Astounding Man."[7]

David Morehouse, in his book *The Complete User's Manual for Coordinate Remote Viewing*, mentions on page 20 that the post-war Remote Viewing programs conducted by the American government were a direct follow-on from the *"very bizarre programs initiated by the Nazis during World War II."*[8]

There has always been a strong thread of interest in the paranormal in Germany and Hitler, along with many of his highest ranking officers, was a participant in secret societies that explored all aspects of the paranormal. During his reign of power, Hitler quietly supported all types of 'occult' activity and his agency during the war years was nicknamed the Occult Bureau by the British.

The correct name for this group was the Ahnenerbe SS and they were involved in everything from cultic ceremonies in costume *"with mystical diagrams and pagan rituals in ruined castles"*[9] to a full spectrum of psychic and paranormal activity.

A significant escalation of activity amongst the Ahnenerbe was the direct result of one of their own practitioners, Ludwig Straniak, who, using only a pendulum on a string, was able to use his psychic abilities to determine the precise location on a map of the two most important ships in the German naval fleet, the *Bismarck* and the *Prinz Eugen*. Officers of the Ahnenerbe SS must have been horrified by Straniak's accuracy as they realised that if they had practitioners capable of targeting locations or items that precisely, it was highly likely that the British military forces had their own 'viewers' who were watching the Germans and compiling reports.[10]

The man in charge of the top-secret institute was Captain Hans A. Roeder of the German Navy. His 'crew' on this astral voyage was composed of specialists in every field from astronomy and astrology to ballistics and spiritualism. The top priority of this motley accummulation of psychics and scientists was the location of enemy ships. [11]

The German government, and the Ahnenerbe SS in particular, were right to be concerned about what the British were doing and it is rumoured that Prime Minister Churchill called his competing group the British Occult Bureau just to have a bit of a dig at Hitler. There was also an American psychic spying group which operated in the 1940s which was reputed to be named The Watch, but I have found it very difficult to find much information about this particular group and I suspect that the activities of those early 'watchers' have been folded into the current intelligence agencies of the USA's government.

All of these recent discoveries simply serve to reinforce in me the understanding that no matter how movie-like the dream or vision might be, complete with elaborate plots, period clothing, and technicolor scenery, my visions are usually quite accurate and I need to *not* second guess them. However, human nature and personal curiosity being what it is, it was thrilling to find out that those types of incidents did actually happen and the German groups seemed to have been in the forefront of psychic research. Also, although it may well be that it would have embarrassed the post-war governments of Great Britain and the USA to admit that some of their victories were due to the efforts of psychics, those facts are recorded and that work was both valid and valuable.

The Glass Sphere Vision

In this fully-awake vision, I saw a man sitting at some sort of console similar to a mockup of a fighter plane simulator in which pilots would train for combat. He was wearing very plain khaki-coloured trousers, much like the bottom half of a military uniform, but he wore no shoes and socks and he was bare-chested. His chest and arms were wired with medical-type electrodes, but there were none on his head or neck. In front of him on the surface of the console was something that appeared to be a clear box made out of some sort of high-impact plastic. The box itself was quite plain and it was closed-in on all sides except for the one open side that was right in front of the man's face. I also noted that there were some sort of thin, gold-like filaments leading from the bottom of the box into the control panel of the console.

A cluster of men and women, perhaps eight in all, watched from an observation platform that was elevated approximately two and one-half metres above the floor of the console where the test subject was sitting. A very thick layer of glass curved around the wall of this semi-circular observation room and that glass was all that separated them from the test subject. Should they need to reach him, the man in the chair below could only be reached through a door that was downstairs in that space where he sat at the console.

There was a very tense atmosphere and the body language of several of the observers appeared to be almost fearful. Down below though, the test subject sat calmly in the chair facing the console and he appeared to be quite unworried about what was about to transpire.

One of the men in the upper deck spoke quietly into the microphone of the headset that he had on and the test subject below heard it through a speaker in his chamber. The bare chested man shook his arms slightly, leaned forward in the chair the tiniest bit, and picked up an object that I had not noticed prior to this time. It was the size of a large marble and appeared to be a clear glass sphere.

Placing the sphere between the thumb and forefinger of his right hand, he moved his left hand onto the console and touched a lever on the flat surface. As he let his left index finger slowly glide on that lever and move it from the bottom to the top, he simultaneously released the glass sphere and it wafted on air into the clear cube and disappeared.

There was a sensation of collective breath-holding as the observers and that man at the console watched the clear box to see if the glass sphere would reappear. After waiting less than sixty seconds, the man at the console reversed the movement of his index finger on the lever and something began to materialise in the air. But instead of returning as a solid marble-sized glass sphere which he could hold between two fingers once again, what came back from the box was a shower of small glass shards. Something on the other side of where the sphere had been sent had smashed it to pieces.

One woman in the upper deck visibly shuddered as she saw the fragments falling all over the surface of the console and I immediately heard her thoughts appear like a sound track in my brain. "What if that had been his head! What if we had allowed another one to try and lean forward to see what was in that time, only to have him fall back in the chair as a headless corpse!"

I could sense the agitation in the room and I realised that this was an ongoing set of experiments and that not all of the 'test subjects' had returned safely. At that moment it occurred to me to pay attention to what those observers were wearing and I instantly recognised clothing from the 1950s. Every one of the five men and three women were dressed the same way that my parents did during my childhood in the 1950s.

The Decade Between

The images that I 'saw' for the period from the mid-1950s through the mid-1960s were quite briefly glimpsed and many of them were distressing to watch. In several locations around the world including in some of the laboratories of quite prestigious universities, experimentation continued to see if men could see into another period of time or into another world altogether that may have existed in a parallel time or on another world.

Animals were placed in cages and launched through various types of devices that were meant to return them to the laboratory a mere few minutes later. But most of the time the cage would never return or it would come back with the bloody corpse of a mangled or exploded animal. On a few rare occasions in those early years, the animal did actually return. But they all died within hours or days of their voyage and every single animal exhibited signs of mental instability.

The Transporter Effect

When I go to the movies or rent a dvd, I always pay attention to how accurately the wardrobe department or costume designer has been in their portrayal of any particular time period. If you happen to turn on the television without consulting the schedule in the newspaper and you hear the opening music and see the characters appear, within seconds before the first dialogue spills from their lips, you can usually ascertain the time period in which the show is meant to be set by simply looking at the clothing that the characters are wearing.

The same thing applies to any of my visions and dreams that are straightforward and factual. These just-the-facts dreams have a very different 'feel' and purpose than the more common psychological-processing dreams that we all have that assist us to comprehend and assimilate our daily world. This next vision appears to show an incident that occurred in the 1960s.

I remember the 1960s well since I entered my teen years just as the floodgates of change were opened and a steady stream of radically different fashion, hair, music, and social attitudes washed over the world. The characters of this vision were all garbed in 1960s clothes with the exception of the three men and two women in the control booth who were in medical-style lab coats. Each of the other personnel manning the controls in that control booth were wearing generic military-style khaki clothing with no insignias or sewn-on patches to indicate what unit they were assigned to. But the bulk of the staff who worked outside that booth in the offices and labs of the ugly post-war concrete building were all dressed in various versions of 1960s clothing and footware.

The day felt hot and the primary character, the man who was about to be the test subject, had longish and fashionably shaggy hair and he wore flared jeans, a rather bright striped shirt, and he had leather sandals on his feet. He looked quite young, perhaps in his early twenties, and there was a canvas bag overflowing with books at the edge of the sofa where he sat, reading a book, taking notes, and waiting. I had a strong sensation that he was studying for his exams as he waited to be called into the laboratory. But then I had a sudden chill that ran through my body as if I knew that he would never leave that building and take those exams.

A brown-cased speaker was mounted up near the ceiling of the room and a voice suddenly crackled from it calling out the young man's name and telling him to report to the laboratory downstairs in the basement. He stood up quickly, jammed the books into the canvas bag before picking it up, and walked briskly out the door and down the hall to the elevator and descended to the floor below. Two guards in plain uniforms stood at the door to the hallway that was directly across from the elevator doors and he gave them a slip of paper that allowed him to pass through.

It was a long hallway with another guard at the far end. As he passed through another heavy metal door, he entered a second long hallway with only one plain door at the end of it—a dull gray door painted with the word LABORATORY.

As he trundled through those passageways, he couldn't have known that he was entering a separate wing that was entirely shielded with lead since the bump-out for that laboratory addition was hidden within an enclosed courtyard that was invisible from the street. As he finally entered the all-white laboratory, he dropped the canvas book bag onto a small metal cart at the side of the door, and walked forward towards the waiting lab technicians.

They were standing in front of a large metal pod with a ship-like hatch for a door. The pod, which looked quite like the space capsules which orbited the Earth with human astronauts as passengers, sat atop a metal cradle that appeared to be able to rock back and forth. As the young man walked up to them, two of the three uniformed men began to clip wires onto his clothing and next they attached two microphones to those wires. Finally, they slid his arms into a canvas-strapped harness, buckled it tightly, and moved the two microphones so that they were now sitting outside the harness. The two shoulder straps each had a small metal slot where something was meant to be coupled and snapped into place and those two somethings were held in the hands of the third uniformed man who now stepped forward and handed the objects to the other two lab technicians. The objects that slid into the metal slots and were clamped into place were two small but quite heavy cameras. The final step was to attach more wires to those cameras. All four men then turned and looked up at a blank section of concrete wall behind which sat the control room and the staff who were giving instructions over the speakers.

After they listened and nodded for a few seconds, one of the uniformed men placed a set of large earphones, with more dangling wires, onto the young man's head just as all four men in the lab turned toward the open hatch door. The test subject waited as two of the technicians carefully draped the wires for all of the equipment over his arms and then he stepped inside, turned back around to face the door, and sat on a small metal stool which was riveted to the floor of the pod. As he sat down, making sure to keep the wires across his arms free and loose, one of the three uniformed men slowly squeezed in beside him and began attaching each of those wires to a connector on the control panels inside the pod. It took several minutes to secure the wires as he maneuvered in the tiny space on either side of the test subject, but when he was done he patted the young man on the shoulder, stepped out, and he closed the hatch door tightly behind him. Within less than a minute, all three of the uniformed men had left the room, gone down the long hallway, and were safely out of distance from the experiment that was about to begin.

The tiny lights of the instruments cast a pale glow onto the face of the young man inside the pod and he waited quietly as he listened to instructions over the internal speakers which told him to speak aloud so that the control room could register his voice output. Within the windowless control room, they could hear the young man clearly and see two images of the hatch in front of him as they were broadcast from the cameras clamped atop his shoulder harness. Another camera had been installed within the pod and they were also able to see his face clearly on a third screen. The monitors in another section of the control room showed images of the now empty lab below and verified that the staff members had indeed left the room. Everything was ready and it was time to begin.

One of the female scientists in the control room leaned forward and spoke soothingly into the microphone, telling the young subject to try and be as calm and clear as possible, no matter what he saw. She emphasised that his observations were vital to science and vital for the future of humankind. He had believed what they told him when they explained that a future home for the citizens of Earth would soon be needed and that it was essential to know if there were hospitable worlds nearby. He nodded quietly and said that he was ready.

Sitting at the control panel within that observation booth, the khaki-clad men began to flick a series of metallic switches upwards into the ON position. Tiny lights on the panel lit up with each new switch that was activated but, other than the nervously audible breathing of some of the staff and the high-pitched humming from the fluorescent bulbs overhead, the room was entirely silent. When the last of the switches had been activated and the single large dial had been turned all the way to the far right position, they collectively held their breath, watched the monitors, and waited.

Within the pod, the young man sat quietly and fretted oh-so slightly about how tightly the harness straps had been done-up and how heavy the cameras on his shoulders already felt. He heard nothing. He felt nothing. Then as the lights on his control panel began to come on and correspond to the switches being activated in the observation room, he felt the tiniest tingling on the surface of his skin as if a blast of cold air had somehow made its way into that sealed chamber. In minute increments, the tingling escalated and then stopped suddenly just at the moment when the young man realised that there was no feeling in any part of his body.

Inside the observation room, the entire group held their breath as they watched the monitor which showed his face and then showed a completely empty pod as he disappeared. They waited for him to return within the allotted sixty seconds of the test, some of them praying silently to themselves, but his face never reappeared. Minutes ticked by and no one moved until the head scientist finally shuffled his feet and cleared his throat. The switches were left on, the dial turned fully up, but in unison they began to busy themselves with making notations and preparing to leave the room. One uniformed staff member stayed behind, staring at the screen with hopeful intent, as the others walked out of the room, locked it behind them, and went upstairs into a conference room for a debrief.

The coffee pot in the conference room had been freshly filled and they each slumped into a chair except for the head scientist who paced the room for a minute before sitting down. Finally one young man said aloud what most of them were thinking. "We cannot keep recruiting these kids! What's worse—losing them to God knows where, not knowing if they survived the trip, or having pieces of them come back like the old animal tests? How can we keep doing this when we have only gotten an occasional monkey back intact?"

No one answered. The room was silent as they stared at their notes.

A Few Conclusions

You will note that I have not included any visions of contemporary attempts to bridge time and space or travel to alternative universes. These few statements that follow are all that I will say on those subjects.

The work continues in earnest and is so well-funded that several small countries could have one-hundred percent of their operating costs covered for years on the annual budget of this research alone. The 'doors and gates' to time and space, as the Dreamkeeper used to refer to them, have long ago been broken through and are being accessed constantly by both curious humans and visitors from other places who are aware that our world is no longer locked-up-tight. I have chosen quite intentionally to *not examine* the details of what is going on and I am sure that the reader can understand that there are safety concerns behind that reluctance.

The human 'time travellers' never slip into another world completely unnoticed and they always leave a residual energy in that other place. But they too have a price to pay upon their return because their life-span is drastically shortened as a result of their back and forth journeying.

On each and every occasion of time movement forward, backward, or simply through, it activates a principle of reciprocity and those on the other side *expect* to be allowed through as well. I strongly believe that this is why we hear of more and more 'odd events' such as people or things disappearing in plain sight or appearances of strange people or objects that have no context in our world.

The other area of strong concern is that the edges of those openings never fully 'heal' or close back tight. This is due to our current level of technology which is quite primitive compared to what operates on the other side. Our doors and gates are 'leaking' and if you liken it to the air pressure within the cabin of a spacecraft that is flying at a great altitude, we could simply explode in a shower of sparkles in the blink of an eye if we continue to play around with these flawed devices. We could literally be the undoing or ourselves.

These scientists and agencies are quite driven, however, and even knowing the possible threat, they continue their day-to-day experiments with this equipment. One of the many examples of this technology that exerts a strong pull on the time-space gates is the project known as HAARP. No matter what you are told that it is, it is not that explanation that is 'officially' and falsely given. It *is* a time-space manipulator! The about-to-go-live CERN experiments in Switzerland are another type of device with the same purpose.

Stepping Out

There is another way of 'stepping out' of the body and out of our time and it does not require the use of any sort of mechanical device. It also leaves no rips in the fabric of time. Before we discuss that though, be aware that the means of moving through time and space that are being employed by world governments and intelligence agencies are not this gentle, natural method.

Time and again they use machine-based technology that they have *developed with the intentional assistance* of travellers from the other time-space realms who have their own agenda for this planet. For years you may have heard theories that everything from early rocket ships to stealth bombers were derived from reverse-engineered devices that were 'captured' from crashed UFOs. But consider how much more sinister it would be if this technology was freely offered by those 'other beings' and it continued, decade after decade, to be 'spoon fed' to the eager humans who failed to comprehend that they were making agreements that could result in the eventual downfall of humans as a species.

Those 'other beings' have never all come from outer space—in many instances they have come from inner space—from the room next door, so to speak. They have existed alongside us and have occasionally chosen to interact with our species when the seeds for a long-term plan were being sewn. They have chosen to share *just enough* information with the human time travel experimenters that, instead of becoming lost in space and time on their time travelling voyages, they can now return to the point of origin.

If, for example, they left a laboratory setting in New Mexico in June of the year 2009, they would be able to return to that same room on the same day and *within the same timeline universe* instead of returning to another almost identical laboratory on the same day in a parallel universe. Unintentionally, those parallel universes were the end of the road for many of the first Earth-human time travellers and other versions of themselves returned to the laboratory of origin here on Earth instead.

What the 'other beings' failed to include in the 'Time Travel Instruction Book' was the method for departing and entering this time-space reality without causing those rips in the fabric that I discussed earlier. That omission was quite intentional. Although it does not apply to all of the 'other beings' that we have discussed, *some of them* have big plans for how to remake our ruined planet for their own purposes or how to harvest the breathtaking amount of energy that would be dispersed if the planet dissolved in a burst of sparkling light. Those agencies and governments, who could potentially be responsible in our near future for exploding our planet with their ill-thought-out experiments that are primitive in contrast to the technology of the 'other beings', contain many scientists and researchers who would never hesitate to step through a door or gate within time and save themselves at the last minute. I have no doubt that they have contingency plans in place for themselves and their loved ones should these risky experiments continue unabated.

Now, to counter that little 'horror story' of what goes on behind the scenes whilst ordinary people live out their lives in complete ignorance, let's discuss the means for time travel that are gentle, natural, harmless to the atmosphere of your planet, and harmless to yourselves individually and as a species. These methods have been known for millennia by a few select individuals who devoted themselves to inner searching and a deeply spiritual path.

In some more recent cases, the methods have been discovered by accident by the curious of mind who found themselves poring over ancient texts and, without meaning to, absorbing those accounts of the 'ancient adepts' who could dematerialise and rematerialise at will or bi-locate to another spot on the planet, perhaps many miles from where they began. Some of these discoveries have been made by spiritual seekers who were also dedicated scholars. Since the task of wading through many of the religious writings of the ages is quite daunting, only the most persistent researcher would continue on the path until they gleaned the knowledge that they sought, knowledge which was often quite intentionally hidden within obscure language.

One such method involves working with one's own subtle energy. People who utilise energy field therapy for healing or those who consciously engage their energy meridians during spiritual practice have an untapped potential simply waiting to be accessed. We have the ability to create an invisible energy spiral that spins around each meridian point and from each chakra. The energy fields that are emitted from each point overlap into a spiderweb shape that criss-crosses back and forth across the body again and again and again like the energy grid of a large city. With calmness and patience, those spirals and webs can pulse and pulse until, suddenly, a silent-sound explodes and an opening appears through which a person can step into another time-space reality. And if they have engaged in this activity with purposeful and ethical intent, they are anchored in this time and space should they choose to return to it.

I find it funny to see just how often the concepts of time travel are being addressed now in movies and on television shows. But in every instance that I have seen thus far, they rely solely on mechanical means to move the human subjects and there are always consequences such as physical effects or dimensional strangeness to overcome. How much more gentle, simple, and effective is the means described above!

Caution Required

I would like to conclude this chapter with a caution for those who might be inclined to want to know more about current 'secret' research such as that hinted at above. I debated whether or not to include this last item, but as 'conspiracy theory' as it might sound, it is all quite true.

Just as I was completing this chapter I stopped to sip my tea and ponder why I was having so many nights of disturbed sleep lately. Was it due to my consciousness processing the occasionally unpleasant subject matter that I have been reviewing, or was it originating from an entirely external source? As fast as that question rolled through my mind, the answer came back from a voice in my head.

Energy signatures from people 'of interest' can now be read by other humans as either a visual image or a radio signal and those signatures are tracked in sophisticated computers. When those computers light up and acknowledge that something 'interesting' is transpiring with people like Deborah, the signals alert 'the watchers' and they suddenly turn that dark attention and intent upon us.

They can create fatigue and brain fog. They can create pain and distress that is quite real. They can insert their 'movies' into your head at night, just as we do.

Shivers!

Chapter Six
HUMAN AND ANIMAL ENGINEERING

It began simply, didn't it? The reason for using animal parts in human bodies was due to long waiting lists for items such as heart valves and skin grafts. What if genetic engineering could create custom vaccines or other medications specifically tailored to work with your own unique DNA? But something much more complex now sits at your door, waiting to enter and make itself at home before you even have a chance to evaluate whether it is advisable to allow the 'creature' to come in.

Approximately 15 years ago, I was doing a series of monthly lectures at a huge warehouse-sized metaphysical bookstore here in Australia and during one of my sessions, I began to talk about the emergence of creatures in the not too distant future that would be such strange hybrids that they would make the creatures of mythology look like cuddly stuffed animals. Everyone laughed nervously, but they knew that I was quite serious about what I was seeing for the future.

The other area of concern that I have had for most of the last two decades is the rise of machine life. I was never worried about straightforward robotic creations, but I kept visualising the merging of robotic beings with aspects of human DNA or consciousness. I mentioned this to a few friends and they told me it sounded as implausible as a science fiction movie.

There have been many, many writers of that particular genre during the 20th century and I must admit that I have never been a reader of science fiction in spite of urgings by my son, the self-professed sci-fi geek, or by friends who regarded it as a style of writing that was as worthy of respect as classical literature. I understood that and I honoured their choices, but each and every time I would pick up a sci-fi book from the shelves of a bookstore, I would hear my own voice saying quietly in my head, "You don't need that." After a bit of analysis, I have concluded that my own mind was rejecting that type of reading material because it was too close to the truth in some cases, and it might subtly influence the nature or accuracy of the visions that I receive.

Several years ago, I was on the phone with my girlfriend Angela who lives in Pennsylvania and is a college professor in theatre arts and the humanities. We've been friends since graduate school and I trust her to give me an honest response to any topic.

What I shared with her that day were some startling news reports that I had read from sources as diverse as the New York Times and the BBC online. The articles that really concerned me were those discussing the merging of human and machine consciousness in laboratories in the USA and I actually gasped aloud when I read them. As I related this to Angela, she shrieked into the phone, "Haven't any of these people ever seen the movie Terminator!" I answered back that if we were seeing little news bursts in mainstream publications, that meant that the governments of the world were 'priming' us to accept these creatures and that the research has probably been going on for far longer than the few years stated in the articles.

Let's discuss a series of visions relating to the 'blending' of humankind with robotics. This might sound all too fanciful at the moment, but just think back a few years ago to when you first heard about devices and situations that you never could have imagined and which have now come into being. A similar trajectory is unfolding for cyborgs and these 'creations' *will* begin to manifest shortly.

The visions that I have had take place within a five to ten year timeframe, but I clearly believe that the technology already exists and is active and functional in laboratory settings. This technology will 'learn' and improve with each variation of the creatures that are created.

As I began to type up this portion of the chapter, I laid back with my eyes closed, did a conscious meditation, and asked for a waking vision on this subject. I saw the world in a not-too-distant future since the clothing and cars looked much the same as today—but the surrounding scenery looked as if it was in a permanent state of neglect and disrepair. There was also a strong sensation that the total population of the planet had been drastically reduced through some disaster or another and that the people who remained were living a less than healthy lifestyle with polluted air, food, and water. Walking amongst these survivors were several men and women with a slightly different gait to their walk—as if they had not progressed through the normal human developmental stages of crawling, toddling, then walking. And their bodies appeared to be glowingly healthy compared to the other people.

These 'unique ones' were not entirely human—that was what the voice in my head told me. Their human consciousness and memories had been removed from their original human body and placed into the clean, new, disease-impervious shell of an artificial life form—a robot. And every single one of these robot-humans worked for some agency of a world dominating government. Interestingly, there was quite a strong life-force energy emitting from each of them and the remaining humans on Earth seemed to have a flickering life-force energy that was weak and diminished.

The next scene that I saw was on another planet—not on Earth—and I have no idea whether it was our own solar system or a different one reached via the by-then-common method of black hole jumping. In this vision, the few totally-human settlers stayed safely within the artificial atmosphere of the domed city. If they ventured outside the dome into the intense heat and light and unbreathable air, they were not only encased in space suits, they were also in vehicles that generated a protective energy field around them. These humans were equal in number to the robot-humans who also lived in the city.

Walking on the surface, seemingly immune to the planetary effects, were other versions of the robot-humans that were not quite so glossy and perfect. On this strange new planet, many of the robot-humans that lived outside the dome were not as 'pretty' to look at and were built for their ability to toil with very little rest, not for their aesthetic appearance or ability to blend in with the small percentage of pure humans that dwelt within the city. Just like the humans on the damaged Earth, these more functional robot-humans had very little spark to their life-force energy. I cannot say that I sensed any hopelessness or despair about the conditions under which they lived and worked—it was more of a blankness that was devoid of emotions.

The other 'worker creatures' on this planet were versions of animals that we now see on Earth, but I knew as I stared at them that they too had been infused with human consciousness and that the reason for their creation had been solely as beasts of labour for the ruling class of pure-humans and robot-humans. There was a sad dullness to most of their life-force energy. But there were the occasional and quite interesting 'sparky' ones that would have developed in ways that were unintended by their creators.

I moved forward in time several generations and discovered that the pure-humans were now considered an oddity— like animals in a zoo. Amongst themselves, they may have considered their pure-humanness to be a rare and wonderful quality to be treasured. But the robot-humans clearly regarded the pure-humans as something quaint and frail.

Leaving the future-visioning and moving back to the here and now...

In light of the above vision, what is equally as worrying to me as the human-machine blending are the reports of human and animal hybrids. I've continued to send articles, some of which I will include below, to a handful of close friends over the last decade and listening to their reactions has reinforced to me that I am not being at all alarmist to fret about these issues.

It would appear that little consideration has been given to the reactions of ordinary people and you have to wonder *why* these scientists have begun to create these monstrosities. They may proclaim that it's all in the interest of scientific exploration or disease research, but what are the implications for the world at large and for the potential creatures themselves? Are these scientists already aware of Earth's fate and working toward the scenario that I described in the waking vision above?

For the time being, the press releases all seem to indicate that the laboratory work is at the cell level and embryos, for example, are not being allowed to grow and develop. But do you really believe that?

In the 1990s when cloning of animals was first discussed, it originally sounded as if it was all a theory that would never be acted on for any concrete purpose and the 'creations' would stay in the lab. However, less than a decade later there are media reports like the one excerpted below describing cloned animals such as cattle and sheep being raised for human consumption.

Even more eerie is this thought. If the hybrid animals being created have been designed as a food source, do we really want to be eating something that is even partially a human?

Is This Cow A Human-Animal Hybrid?

A Dutch biotechnology company called Pharming has genetically engineered cows, outfitting females with a human gene that causes them to express high levels of the protein human lactoferrin in their milk. According to Pharming's website, "the protein, which is naturally present in human tears, lung secretions, milk and other bodily fluids, fights against the bacteria that causes eye and lung infections, plays a key role in the immune system of infants and adults and improves intestinal microbial balance, promoting the health of the gastro-intestinal tract. Since the protein has the ability to bind iron, is a natural anti-bacterial, anti-fungal and anti-viral, is an antioxidant and also has immunomodulatory properties, large groups of people might benefit from orally administered lactoferrin," the company literature reads. [12]

Moving forward to the latest items in the news that discuss human and animal combinations, we have certainly leapt into what I perceive to be another potentially dangerous area for humankind.

For all of the assertions by the scientists who are being interviewed that this type of research is meant to enhance life or halt such devastating diseases as cancer, Parkinson's, Huntington's, and Multiple Sclerosis, there will always be less than ethically inclined researchers with no such lofty goals. It is those scientists and researchers that cause worry. How will an artificially created animal-human hybrid act or react if they are allowed to grow past the test-tube stage into a full being and begin to develop a human-like consciousness?

The sole intent of the scientists in question may be to create a type of 'Super Human' that can be utilised in special operations military forces. Or, as mentioned in the waking vision, perhaps they wish to design a combination of human and animal that has the best characteristics of each species and which is designed for some sole purpose like underground or off planetary physical labour. But evolving sentient life forms may eventually have other ideas of how to live their lives once they become fully conscious and I find very little evidence in the published literature that those concerns are being addressed.

Any future assertions that may be forthcoming about how they 'have it all under control' will fall on deaf ears as far as I am concerned. There is no way to create any entirely new and completely artificial life form that will not 'escape' its masters and either act in unpredictable ways, develop disease transmission issues, potentially exhibit unstable or dangerous behaviour, mate with creatures that they were not meant to mate with, or mutate into another life form that was never pre-planned.

Having said all of that, how often as you have read this book has the thought occurred to you, as it often has to me, that the writers of science fiction for the past several decades were either extremely prescient or were mental time travellers of a sort that echoes current remote viewing methods.

UK's first hybrid embryos created

By Fergus Walsh: Medical correspondent, BBC News

Scientists at Newcastle University have created part-human, part-animal hybrid embryos for the first time in the UK, the BBC can reveal. [13]

If this type of research has already been unleashed and they are allowing tiny snippets of fact-based information to be introduced to the public, trust me, they will not be reversing course and suddenly deciding that those were doors that were best left closed. Now that the scientists who are doing this research have achieved a measure of success, they will continue to push the boundaries of what they are able to accomplish even if the rest of the non-scientific world has objections or concerns regarding the nature of the work or even the wisdom of attempting such things.

And what are we to think of creatures that are brought to life from the quantum realm? In this September 2009 article in *New Scientist* magazine, those possibilities are posed.

Quantum weirdness could soon invade the living world, if a scheme to give a flu virus a strange double life comes off. [14]

The online version of the article contains a picture of a 'water bear' that has been created in the quantum realm and indeed, it does have a strong resemblance to a bear. But equally as interesting as the article were the over four dozen comments offered by the readers of the magazine, many of whom were as startled by this revelation as I was. Is it wise to continue to create new life forms simply because we have the ability to *do* so?

Chapter Seven
THE ENEMIES OF THE STATE

I am fortunate that I not only have an excellent recall of time periods, but I have also kept either a written journal or have done significant online posting for the last two decades. I am therefore able to pinpoint when I first had a vision about this subject.

A series of events that I had foreseen over fifteen years ago are now escalating in a most alarming manner—the waging of warfare on humankind by other humans. And in this case, I am not referring to out-and-out declared wars or ethnic conflicts, battles for territory or oil or fishing rights, arguments over natural resources, or any other so-called tangible issues that can be determined at present. What I am about to discuss is the redistribution of power and the intentional psychological programming that allows empire-like governments to look upon individual citizens as something less than beings with the right and freedom to live their lives in peace.

It is my firm belief, as stated in my previous book, that a plan is now under way to reduce the global human population by a variety of means. Some of these are quite subtle and the population reduction can be written off to personal choices made by individuals. But in other cases which I will outline below, any rational person who is living in a so-called civilised society will have to ask why technology is being developed that clearly operates from a viewpoint of humans as a disposable commodity.

There are many sources both online and in print which can outline the master plan of the Puppet Masters who are creating this scenario, so I will not be dwelling on who-and-why in this book. What may have seemed like 'conspiracy theory' weirdness to many people even a decade ago is gradually becoming accepted by larger segments of the population as they wake up from their numb acceptance of anything that the government or 'the official experts' tell them and they finally begin to think for themselves.

A simple web search of the following key phrase will be quite an eye opener. After typing "intentional population reduction" into an online search engine, it returned 982,000 results in less than 30 seconds.

There are many previously published documents both in print and online regarding the following topics which are forms of warfare against humankind: genetically modified food which reduces or destroys the body's own immune system, publicly acknowledged 'weather wars' by the most powerful nations, intentionally created diseases, and inoculations for those intentionally created diseases that can actually kill you instead of cure you. Due to the wealth of existing material on those topics, I will touch lightly on those subjects and primarily focus on the robotic or technology related inventions that are already present in the world which are clearly aimed at causing serious bodily damage or death to anyone who protests the inequities of the world or who happens to be a named 'enemy' of any particular country.

All of these subjects are sobering things to read. But I consider these facts to be a part of your own personal 'wellness bag' if you are able to incorporate this knowledge into your lives and avoid contact with any or all of the above simply by being informed and alert.

Food That Kills

What better way to reduce a large percentage of the global population than to create food and water that is so unfit to consume that it actually damages or destroys the immune system so that some people die a lingering death, unaware that what they have eaten has contributed to their state of illness. What if this plan includes the genetic manipulation of crops, animals being be fed those altered crops, and, eventually, such tainted food being consumed by humans—thus passing even more contamination into our species.

The variety of sources for food contamination, including substances percolating up through the soil and the bottom of the ocean floor, was addressed quite thoroughly in my previous book, *The Dreamkeeper Messages,* so I will not detail all of those matters again. Part of what is unfolding right now as disease escalates or new 'syndromes' arise is the end result of half a century of conscious pollution and the heretofore previously unknown and unseen effects of ingested chemical residue and toxins in combination with the polluted food, water, and air on this planet.

We must each take individual responsibility for the substances that we ingest, but a great percentage of us were quite ignorant of the long-term effects of those chemical combinations mentioned above until quite recently. The 'lowering-the-threshold' of food safety appears to be either ignorance, corporate greed, a planned process of intentionally thinning out the human species, or a combination of all of those factors.

A May 2009 report by the American Academy of Environmental Health states,

> *Therefore, because GM foods pose a serious health risk in the areas of toxicology, allergy and immune function, reproductive health, and metabolic, physiologic and genetic health and are without benefit, the AAEM believes that it is imperative to adopt the precautionary principle, which is one of the main regulatory tools of the European Union environmental and health policy and serves as a foundation for several international agreements.* [15]

The rapid increase in immune system disorders, toxicity and allergy to foods that had previously not existed in individuals, and a rise in both obesity and infertility are all beginning to be linked back to our consumption of GMO foods. Add to that the amount of excreted pharmaceutical products that are in the water sources of many major cities in the world, the chemicals that are then added to the water to 'clean them up' and you are increasing the levels of toxicity that our individual bodies are attempting to process.

There are, thankfully, more and more physicians and scientists coming out and openly proclaiming that this is a potential ticking time-bomb for the human species and that it is long past time to wind this process back. But is that even doable given how profitable the medical industry, the pharmaceutical industry, and the GMO industries have become? Since all three of those groups can afford to spend vast amounts of dollars lobbying the governments of the world to allow them to do as they wish, unhampered by the objections of citizen-consumers who are worried about these negative health trends, how can the genie ever be put back into the bottle?

This chilling statement from the website of a law firm in South America makes it quite clear that the health departments of various governments of the world, agencies which should be tasked with keeping our food and water safe, are simply not doing that.

> To begin with it's important to understand that there is no special regulatory system for GM foods. The FDA has determined that no safety studies will be necessary. So who does decide if the GMOs produced by the Biotech Corps are harmful or fit for consumption by humans and animals? The answer is the industry itself. [16]

Just how many chemicals from food, air, water, and vaccinations can our bodies ingest without becoming toxic soup? It is highly unlikely that the manufacturers of these substances have done extensive testing on the outcome of combining them. And just because a substance is safe and effective under certain conditions, who is to say that it will not cause great damage to the body when combined with the other frequently encountered chemicals and the novelty ones such as seasonal vaccines. What is the long term outcome for us as a species if we reduce our cognitive functions, destroy our ability to reproduce, escalate episodes of dementia, and create life-threatening allergies?

Intentionally Created Diseases and Inoculations That Damage or Kill

In a quite recent example, within hours after hearing that the so called 'Swine Flu' or H1N1 flu was expected to become a pandemic and that a behind-the-scenes plan was already in play for massive, global inoculations to be administered, my body reacted immediately with a strong resonance of disbelief. I am thoroughly convinced that what I heard on the news that day was a well-fabricated story to 'sell' the masses on the importance of believing in the fantasy and allowing themselves to be given spurious medication that could actually damage their bodies instead of healing them.

Mere days later, a few brave media reporters began to state the same thing and within weeks there was a strong groundswell against a sheep-like belief in this concocted pandemic. It has been pointed out in several on-air news reports that it is ludicrous for the WHO, the World Health Organization, to have already declared this situation to be a pandemic when thus far it is actually causing less fatalities than arise during a run of normal flu in any routine year.

So who benefits by this 'spin' being placed on the so-called 'killer flu'? What purpose does it serve to keep a large population in each country in a state of fear and trepidation? Finally, who would profit by the creation of a disease that then requires a laboratory-created solution?

Other than the vaccine makers, one answer may lie in this 21 September 2009 article from Reuters.

(Reuters)—Shares of VeriChip Corp (CHIP.O) tripled after the company said it had been granted an exclusive license to two patents, which will help it to develop implantable virus detection systems in humans. [17]

A mere month later it was clear that virus detection was not the only agenda for these implantable devices. An

October 2009 article from titled *"Microchip Implant to Link Your Health Records, Credit History, Social Security"* stated the following:

> *Novartis and Proteus Biomedical are not the only companies hoping to implant microchips into patients so that their pill-popping habits can be monitored. VeriChip of Delray Beach, Fl., has an even bolder idea: an implanted chip that links to an online database containing all your medical records, credit history and your social security ID.*
>
> *As this presentation to investors makes clear, the chip and its database could form the basis of a new national identity database lined to Social Security and NationalCreditReport.com.* [18]

There are two areas of concern here—the highly suspect flu itself and the 'chipping' of humans. In my previous book, *The Dreamkeeper Messages,* it was mentioned over a decade ago that devices of some kind would be implanted into humans to track them in the future. That may have seemed a bit 'out there' to my readers back then, but this is now a real-world fact and the future that I saw in the mid-1990s seems to have arrived.

It may well be that, right on schedule, the flu does mutate at some point, but we still have to wonder why the original source material has been analysed and has been found to be a concoction of several types of flu virus that would never be a naturally occurring event. The origin is plainly a laboratory creation, but did it 'escape' from its laboratory confines or was it, as many have suggested, foisted upon a fearful public as a means of either testing human vulnerabilities to this virus cocktail, or population thinning?

From an article in the Wayne Madson Report,

It has also been discovered that suspected ancestor viruses are coming from old isolates. The NA gene comes from a 1996-2001 isolate, the M gene from 1990-1993 isolates, and the others even older, somewhere between 1979 to 1980s isolates. The consensus virologist community contends that the A/H1N1 virus has been in existence for over 20 years without ever being detected. WMR's virologist states that it is impossible for a virus existing for 20 years without being detected given the amount of virus medical surveillance that takes place around the world. [19]

In the earlier segment, I posed the question of how many chemicals the body could accommodate and who, if anyone, was paying attention to the potentially negative interaction between substances in GMO foods and vaccinations. If there are known neurotoxins being pumped into our bodies by a variety of delivery methods, how long will it be before we lose our ability to thrive as a species?

Imagine how stunned I was to discover that food is now considered a viable delivery method for vaccinations! A June 2009 article in Natural News states the following,

GMOs Enable Trojan Horse Vaccinations

Edible vaccines, as GMO foods, are in the future as well. Meat and Poultry, *a business journal for meat and poultry processors, reports in a May 5, 2009 article, by Bryan Salvage, that researchers at Iowa State University are working on creating a method to install vaccines into corn crops.* [20]

On this rare occasion, words simply fail to express my disgust at the information above. Since many countries allow GMO foods to be sold with no labeling to indicates that fact to potential consumers, we may find ourselves more inclined to purchase somewhat more expensive organic foods that clearly bear a label attesting to non-GMO status.

Technology to Kill or Subdue

In an article published in *New Scientist* magazine in March 2008, David Hambling wrote an article titled "US Army Toyed With Telepathic Ray Gun" which revealed the true depths to which that government would sink to use their own citizens as 'guinea pigs' for testing new weaponry.

A recently declassified US Army report on the biological effects of non-lethal weapons reveals outlandish plans for "ray gun" devices, which would cause artificial fevers or beam voices into people's heads. [21]

The specifics of this weaponry are in the ENDNOTES section and I found it quite disturbing to read. I don't think that I am being overly alarmist to say that these types of technologies would be bad enough if we discovered that innocent animals were being used as test subjects, but how much more sinister is it to find that our fellow humans have been subjected to any of what was detailed above?

In another twist on control via technology, a new device developed by a Canadian company, Lamperd, is designed to maintain complete control over airline passengers by a most unusual means.

Lamperd, a 'firearm training system' company, has pat-
ented a bracelet that delivers debilitating shocks when
remotely triggered [by an airline attendant, air marshal
or the pilot]. They are proposing that the TSA [the U.S.A's
Transportation Safety Administration] could force every-
one who flies to wear one of these and then flight-atten-
dants could zap passengers into a stupor if they turn out
to be terrorists. [22]

How many people are going to want to fly under those
kinds of circumstance? And who is going to be responsible
for any 'accidental deaths' when these electrical shocks cause
heart attacks or strokes or epileptic seizures?

A third chilling example of technology run amok—
about robots intentionally designed to hunt down 'unruly'
humans—appeared in an October 2008 article from *New
Scientist.*

Packs of Robots Will Hunt Down
Uncooperative Humans

The latest request from the Pentagon jars the senses. At
least, it did mine. They are looking for contractors to pro-
vide a "Multi-Robot Pursuit System" that will let packs of
robots "search for and detect a non-cooperative human". [23]

Finally, under the being-constantly-observed category,
what should we think about bugs that are NOT bugs?
This excerpt from a *Washington Post* article sounded like
something from a sci-fi movie.

Dragonfly or Insect Spy?
Scientists at Work on Robobugs
By Rick Weiss-Washington Post *Staff Writer*

Vanessa Alarcon saw them while working at an antiwar rally in Lafayette Square last month. "I heard someone say, 'Oh my god, look at those,'" the college senior from New York recalled. "I look up and I'm like, 'What the hell is that?' They looked kind of like dragonflies or little helicopters. But I mean, those are not insects." [24]

For those wishing to explore future possibilities, I offer a pair of links for you to explore. I rarely, if ever, recommend other people's websites or work—not because I am not generous enough to acknowledge that others are making wonderfully unique and valuable contributions, but because at times in the past I have recommended a site or two and then watched as the quality of the work offered declined precipitously. I would hope that this is never the case with these two sites.

Future-visioning is something that frequently is done by people such as myself who are able to place ourselves in an altered state of consciousness and step into another space and time reality for a brief moment. In my own case, what I see comes to me in the form of a movie-like vision.

But what if you were able to predict future events with clarity and accuracy by using a rather sophisticated computer program? That is exactly what Clif High at Half Past Human is doing with some astonishing results. The premise of his work is that we are all psychic to some extent and we give off waves of information in our internet chatter that point to impending events even when we are unaware that we are doing it. The computer program he wrote scans online chatter via webbots looking for linguistic shifts which might portend future events. From this data, he compiles a report that analyses time periods as far as a year into the future. I have been quite impressed with the predictions thus far, hence the recommendation.

http://www.halfpasthuman.com

The second recommendation is for Clif's partner in the work, George Ure. George actually has a financial column online called Urban Survival. He states firmly that he has no financial partnership with Clif so there is no reason for him to hype the reports, but these two men are friends and colleagues and George promotes the work that Clif does quite effectively. A great percentage of George's writing every day is devoted to world trends, small snippets of news that you might miss elsewhere, and putting together bits and pieces of events around the world to form a conclusion or two about where things are heading. He references Clif's work a lot and when you hear radio interviews about the reports, you usually hear both Clif and George discussing them together with the interviewer. George has a wonderfully folksy humour and his site is updated each weekday.

http://urbansurvival.com/week.htm

Chapter Eight
CHALLENGING TIMES

The formerly predictable four seasons of our year, with their accompanying rain, snow, or wind, are acting like volatile strangers and we all now have no choice but to adapt to these new realities. As optimistic as I normally am, I rather doubt that there is any way to reverse the various permutations of Climate Change within our lifetime unless some sort of stunning technology suddenly appears on the horizon that can 'refresh' the land, air and water back to a previous decade. Notwithstanding my fervent desire for such a sci-fi solution, this is now a less than optimistic future that we pass on to our children and grandchildren.

There are many theories about the decline in the quality of life on earth and they range from manmade climate events to overpopulation to cyclical solar effects. I believe that what we are now living through is a combination of all of those plus a drought cycle that will increase the number of deserts worldwide, an upcoming cooling off cycle that will go hand in hand with the global warming, and magnetic effects from our universe that are not yet widely discussed. For this reason, I feel that Global Warming is a much less accurate term than Climate Change. And I believe that the current push to get everyone to think alike on that topic carries its own agenda.

In my view, (a) it is a bit too simplistic to say that the actions of mankind are the sole reason for the decline in Earth's viability as a place to reside, (b) not enough attention is being paid to the fact that some portions of the globe are actually decreasing in temperature instead of increasing, hence the phrase Global Warming is incorrect terminology if it is being applied to the whole of the Earth, (c) more attention needs to be paid to the activity of the Sun as a factor in Climate Change, (d) historical accounts of climate and geological disasters in ancient times are *not* simply mythology and we should be looking to the past for signs to point to our own impending future.

The latest scientific research is discussed in a September 2009 article titled, "Climate Change May Trigger Earthquakes and Volcanoes" and this new research may cause a drastic rethink in what to expect from both weather and geological changes.

As Richard Fisher writes,

Far from being the benign figure of mythology, Mother Earth is short-tempered and volatile. So sensitive in fact, that even slight changes in weather and climate can rip the planet's crust apart, unleashing the furious might of volcanic eruptions, earthquakes and landslides.

That's the conclusion of the researchers who got together last week in London at the conference on Climate Forcing of Geological and Geomorphological Hazards. It suggests climate change could tip the planet's delicate balance and unleash a host of geological disasters. What's more, even our attempts to stall global warming could trigger a catastrophic event. [25]

In my first book, *The Dreamkeeper Messages*, there were chapters filled with descriptions of the visions that I'd been having for decades of a rapid set of changes in the appearance of the planet via unprecedented storms and high winds, tsunamis, geological upheaval, and the alteration of coastlines around the world as the oceans rose precipitously and changed the shape of continents. I had no answers as to why I expected it all to happen and the science of the time offered no explanation. I simply took the visions on faith, transcribed them in my books and online posts, and then hoped that someone would be interested in knowing that these things were in humanity's not-too-distant future. Now, several decades later, there are almost daily revelations from the newest scientific studies which prove that indeed, the face of the planet can be altered in a very short period of time with an accompanying loss of life on a catastrophic scale.

As all of those events have begun to unfold, that first book is now quite timely since it contains footnoted articles that explain my future visions. It is also clear from the article above that the research will need to continually be reevaluated to determine if the correct path is actually being pursued in combating Climate Change.

The insurance industry and local governments in almost every country have recently awakened to the idea that they cannot continue to allow construction of either residential or commercial buildings at the oceanfront since those properties are easily lost to sudden and catastrophic events like hurricanes or rising water levels worldwide. The growing number of tsumanis caused by massive and ever-more-frequent earthquakes in the Pacific Rim's Ring of Fire has made living on a tropical island quite perilous for millions of people.

Places that once were icy cold are becoming balmy and perhaps on the edge of tropical. There are flocks of tropical birds such as parrots and wild parakeets living in the suburbs of London and it is only in recent years that southern England became consistently warm enough for these birds to feel comfortable making their home there.

As the warmth creeps in and the humidity rises in places that were once temperate, diseases such as malaria and fungal infections will be new facts of life to contend with. They will further erode our immune systems which have been compromised by artificially created 'plagues' and filthy air, water, and food. Locations in the world that formerly had moderately hot summer months will unite with the places known for great heat to become so blisteringly oven-like and desolate that it will be the cause of a great loss of life, especially amongst the elderly and the very young.

The populations of every continent are mushrooming, so power supply issues will get incrementally worse each year as those additional people demand more power to combat either extremes of heat or extremes of cold. And regarding those extremes of heat, if you either live in Europe or simply keep yourself informed of global issues while residing elsewhere in the world, you will remember that those killer extremes of heat arrived mid-year in 2003 and took over 50,000 lives.

There have been many articles and books recently that discussed the global agricultural patterns that are now completely altered as crops that were traditionally associated with various regions are no longer able to be grown in those spots or whole new growing belts are emerging in places where the climate was once hostile to the crops in question.

Where Will All the People Go

Another important issue to address is the question of what happens to the refugees from climate change. If coastlines and farmlands, cities and jobs are either washed away or destroyed by a repeated series of weather or geological disasters, where will all of these displaced people go? What countries will be expected to take them in when those same potential host nations may be experiencing their own coastal instability, weather or geological upheaval, crop failures, or decline in animal and sea life used to feed their current population?

It will be a matter of compassion, diplomacy, and instilling a sense of understanding in the citizens of the potential host countries. The hard times befalling the incoming refugees could just as easily have happened to them. But in broaching that discussion, the people of the less challenged nations may also choose to refuse entry to the refugees in an attempt to preserve the way of life that they are comfortable with and the reserves that may be needed to feed, clothe, and care for their own citizens. It is a highly complex issue that may prove to be contentious for both sides and difficult to resolve in an amicable manner.

As a former resident of Europe, I know that there is already a rising resentment regarding the strains being placed on the economic foundations of many countries awash with refugees who have fled war and economic hardship in their native lands. This resentment is bound to be even more pronounced when another wave of 'climate change refugees' pours in.

The medical and social services in Britain alone are close to buckling as the more populated areas experience an unending influx of immigrants and a rise in crime that is perceived to be associated with the shift in demographics. In France, young immigrants have rioted in the suburbs of Paris recently, protesting their sense of alienation from mainstream French culture. They feel passed over when it comes to job and educational opportunities based on the fact that they are not native to France.

These countries are just two examples of a trend that is going to escalate as the shape and stability of continents or island nations changes and the residents of those places have no choice but to flee and resettle. For every one of the nations that knows that they will be asked to host refugees, advance planning must be implemented to allow a smoother transition and less friction between the citizens of the host country and the newcomers.

The World Bank has published a map of Bangladesh, which shows that a 1-meter rise in sea level would inundate half of the country's riceland. It would also displace some 40 million Bangladeshis. Where would these people go? Which countries would be willing to accept even a million refugees fleeing the effects of rising sea level?

World Bank, World Development Report 1999/2000 (New York: Oxford University Press, 2000), p. 100

Chapter Nine

THE TIME BLADE

Please note as you begin this rather disturbing chapter that, aside from this brief preface, the words are all from The Dreamkeeper. I have found examples of the situations that she refers to and have inserted those references within this chapter so that the reader can fully understand what lies ahead. The full extract of each article is in the ENDNOTES section at the back of the book, but each link will lead you to a much longer article which is posted online for each of these subjects. It is worth your time to read them all quite thoroughly so you will understand what she is trying to prepare you for.

From The Dreamkeeper

We begin by finally telling you why there is a conscious plan to reduce the population of the planet. It is a misguided attempt to save the masses from the pain and fear ahead. It is not as simple as believing that the rich and powerful wish to have more for themselves. That is the case in some instances. But like a set of twisted parent figures, the great Puppet Masters who control the assets and finances of your world truly think that they are acting in a benevolent manner and saving humankind from damage by killing them off before that darkness arrives. They have known for decades that what is on the way will prove to be the final unraveling or serious crippling of human life on Earth.

The impending event is not without precedent on your planet, but we will not give you dates for the arrival and there is a reason for that. It matters not when it is coming—but it is not that far in the distance. We wish for you to embrace every day with clarity and joy, not dread. So how would knowing a date or time be helpful in that process?

It has been here before and, after departing your world on this upcoming occasion, it will swing back to revisit this globe at a future date many millennia ahead. We refer to this event in the same way that we did in the past—we call it a Time Blade.

The name itself sounds ominous and in some ways it is an accurate reflection of the nature of the Time Blade. It slices through your time with a clean cut. It severs one version of your history, your past and your present, in a never-to-be-rejoined manner. It forever transforms the appearance of your planet within days as it then it moves on to another point in space. Very little in its path will survive.

You will know that it is coming since there will be announcements in your news media, but there will be no place to hide. We hope that by that point in your not-too-distant future, you will have prepared yourself mentally to rejoin your true self, your soul-self, and you will be less distressed about the potential loss of the physical shell that you call your body.

The animals, both domestic and wild, will become agitated and sense the impending threat long before you are able to see the first manifestations. The skies will darken and it will simply appear to be a thunderstorm. But the severity of the wind will soon create a scouring, broom-like condition that will scrape the face of the planet just before the actual assault begins.

The arrival of the Time Blade on this occasion will again be accompanied by a rain of small ball-shaped objects just ahead of the larger ones that you call asteroids. But whereas in the past there may have been one or two large objects that hit the planet, this time there will be a showering of asteroids, not a mere one or two, and no land mass on your world will remain untouched.

Mid-air explosions will turn bodies into dust and the sheer physical pounding will rip land masses apart, send waves of vapour and pulverized material into the air, and then that acidic material will settle back onto the surface in a densely thick and toxic slime that coats every surface.

We have described the specifics to Deborah and asked her to see if there is written evidence of one of these prior visits of the Time Blade. What she has found is below.

Asteroid Impact Fueled Global Rain of BBs

The asteroid that struck the Yucatan Peninsula 65 million years ago presumably initiated the extinction of the dinosaurs. The huge collision also unleashed a worldwide downpour of tiny BB-sized mineral droplets, called spherules.

The hard rain did not pelt the dinosaurs to death. But the planet-covering residue left behind may tell us something about the direction of the incoming asteroid, as well as possible extinction scenarios, according to new research. The falling spherules might have heated the atmosphere enough to start a global fire, as one example. [26]

Your human governments have long known that the catastrophic impact on your planet by objects from space is not a possibility, it is a fact. The combination of smaller items raining on the surface of Earth and hard hitting impacts from objects like asteroids is well documented in your Earth history as the cause of species extinction in the past. You are about to face that series of events yet again.

The Earth Changes that we spoke of in the previous chapter are the lead up stages to the big show, the arrival of the Time Blade that will reduce the population of Earth's humans to zero or to a mere handful of people sprinkled around the surface of your world.

When you see small articles in your newspapers or other media that indicate that the scientists of your world are discussing objects impacting the planet, know this. If they are finally allowing you to have a slight knowledge of this, it has been something that they have known and been frantically working on for decades. This is not new information. It is simply their way of 'educating' the humans of Earth and of conditioning them ahead of time for what is to come.

This strategy has been mentioned in several locations in this book—the manner in which those in power finally condescend to allow the vast populations of Earth to know the actual truth of their fate and future regarding areas as diverse as weather, space, plagues, human experimentation, alien contact, robotic creatures, and much more. They have created the permanently childlike state that many adults reside in as a result of this type of 'talking down' to the people of this planet.

It is too late for the effects of this 'dumbing down' to be reversed at this point, and we mention this only to explain why it is so difficult for you to get through to family and friends who do not share your mindset about all things spiritual and mystical and prophetic. They may choose to believe that the governments of the world are benevolent bodies that are acting in their best interests because it is far easier for them to accept that 'reality' than to peel back the layers and see the true darkness that lies at the core of this manipulation of information.

The governments of your world are frantically creating new research facilities and weapons which are being launched into space to prevent these events from happening.

Earth is not meant to be a safe haven for humans for much longer. But that is not altogether a bad thing since it will free your soul-lives to rest and then move on to other places and other forms of consciousness. That was indeed the original plan which has been forgotten by your soul-selves each and every time that you opted back into a human body for yet another round of incarnation on this world.

EXCERPT: 109TH CONGRESS—
1ST SESSION H. R. 1022

To provide for a Near-Earth Object Survey program to detect, track, catalogue, and characterize certain near-earth asteroids and comets.

IN THE HOUSE OF REPRESENTATIVES

MARCH 1, 2005

Mr. ROHRABACHER (for himself, Mr. NADLER, and Mr. WEINER) introduced the following bill; which was referred to the Committee on Science. A BILL To provide for a Near-Earth Object Survey program to detect, track, catalogue, and characterize certain near-earth asteroids and comets. Be it enacted by the Senate and House of

Representatives of the United States of America in Congress assembled, [27]

The attempt to fend off the impact of comets and asteroids has resulted in the development of space vehicles that are being launched into space to blow up or change the direction of these objects. It should be apparent by now that many of the films that have been made in the last decade or more about the dangers of asteroids which collide with Earth and cause great loss of life are based on genuine threats. Your world governments have clearly 'leaked' this information in an attempt to condition the minds of people around the world. As a result, the filmmakers who plainly have this 'insider knowledge' are communicating what those threats to humankind are.

Deep Impact

Deep Impact is comprised of two parts, a flyby spacecraft and a smaller impactor. The impactor will be released into the comet's path for the planned high-speed collision. The crater produced by the impactor is expected to range from the width of a house up to the size of a football stadium and be from two to 14 stories deep. Ice and dust debris will be ejected from the crater revealing the material beneath. [28]

And in another article...

Warning Over Stealth Comets

Comets that are invisible to astronomers could pose a lethal threat from space, scientists said yesterday. They believe that giant "stealth" comets made up of loose material reflect so little light that they cannot be seen.

If the theory is right, the chance of the Earth being hit by a comet big enough to wipe out human civilisation may be higher than experts believe. [29]

We have observed that many of the humans in positions of power are operating under the belief that they will be able to preserve some aspects of humanity, some remnant of your civilisation, by either moving into underground cities (many of which have been under construction for decades) or by relocating to other planets.

Great efforts will be made to find planets that are similar to Earth and which can sustain human life. If those options are not available in time, you can expect to see untold amounts of money being spent to create cities that float in space or colonies on planets such as Mars where the entire community would need to be encased in a protective sphere or covering to shield the human residents from the effects of the inhospitable atmosphere and weather. We will now address these options separately.

In the case of the underground city option, those humans and human hybrids that move into underground cities or bunkers will almost all find themselves buried alive or crushed by various types of incoming off-planetary objects.

What we had not mentioned until this time is that the impact of these space objects will cause an escalation in the movements of the overlapping landmass plates that cover the surface of your world. When this plate movement begins, the liquid centre of your planet will shift with dramatic rapidity to gush out of every available opening on the surface and ooze into newly created pockets underground—and those pockets will include the supposedly impenetrable and safe underground cities.

If the full impact from the Time Blade is felt and all efforts to deflect or divert it have failed, the land on every continent will be torn apart, the seas will boil, and the gashed openings, both on the surface and under the sea, will spill forth ancient toxic substances that will blend with the chemical soup that you have created for all these decades with your own rampant pollution.

Asteroid attack: Putting Earth's defences to the test —
23 September 2009

...the US air force recently brought together scientists, military officers and emergency-response officials for the first time to assess the nation's ability to cope, should it come to pass. [30]

Another plan, to flee the planet altogether, is also well past the planning stages and is beginning to surface through articles in the media that are designed to subtly 'indoctrinate' the public into an acceptance of humans living in space as an alternative to life on Earth.

NASA Plans Lunar Outpost: Permanent Base at
Moon's South Pole Envisioned by 2024
By Marc Kaufman: Washington Post Staff Writer
Tuesday, December 5, 2006

NASA unveiled plans yesterday to set up a small and ultimately self-sustaining settlement of astronauts at the south pole of the moon sometime around 2020—the first step in an ambitious plan to resume manned exploration of the solar system. [31]

There will be a growing number of mentions in your daily news of the discovery of new planets that are similar in composition to Earth. Although they may be a great distance from your current home world, there are plans that are well under way for the exploration of these potential outposts as evacuation spots for humankind. The colonies on your Moon and Mars and the cities hanging in space near the Earth are meant to be the first stages of a larger move outward and away from Earth and into new sections of the galaxy and beyond. They are only the first step and permanent occupation of other planets is the long-term goal.

What these articles all fail to note at this early stage is what the Earth explorers will do when they arrive if they encounter occupants of the Earth-like planet which are not interested in sharing their home with the refugees from Earth. Part of your evolution as a species is dependent on your attitude as you reach other worlds. Will humans arrive with an open-hearted and open-minded respect toward any and all existing species on those worlds? Or will they arrive as conquerors?

New 'super-Earth' found in space

Astronomers have found the most Earth-like planet out-side our Solar System to date, a world which could have water running on its surface. [32]

You will note that many solutions are being methodically pursued to prevent the complete elimination of human life on Earth. That is a natural instinct for preservation that we do understand. But there are better things to focus on in your lives.

We would ask you to pay little heed to any of this and instead to turn your attention to life in the here and now by becoming the best possible version of yourself. Joyously immerse yourself in a sense of purpose and allow that energy to carry you forward each day with little thought for the how-long-is-left issue. In that way, you will always arrive at your next destination, no matter when or where the point of departure may be, in a state of loving peace instead of frantic fear.

Chapter Ten
THE HOPEFUL HEART

From The Dreamkeeper

We say all of these things to be intentionally provocative— to make you think about the opportunities for joy that are lost each day but which can be reclaimed. But we also are aware that most of the people who read our words are already in that much smaller percentage of humankind that actually do want to approach life in a more engaged manner.

Some of you will become angry when you read our words about the impending arrival of the Time Blade. You may say to yourselves, either referring to us or to Deborah, "How can she act as if it does not matter if life on this planet is wiped out? If she (the Dreamkeeper) has no body and cannot feel body sensations the way we do, she can't even understand how frightened and angry we feel about losing our lives."

Please remember that we have been here from the earliest beginnings of time. We have seen many species and planets and versions of human-like beings come and go. And yes, there is a sense of regret but also an understanding that it is the natural order of things, As one dominant species or place of occupation expires, another one rises to take the place of the one that has been lost.

We hope that you truly understand and believe that nothing is ever lost and that life for you does go on in another form. To believe that the death of your body is the end of everything is to deny the true nature of yourselves in your larger and more real versions in spirit. That is your true life and this temporary period of wearing the clothes of a human body is a type of dream sensation that tests you and helps you to grow and mature in the spiritual realm. The physical reality that you *believe* that you dwell in has always been an illusion.

For as long as you are here, for as long as you have health and loving companions, there is hope. This life that you lead could cease tomorrow from natural causes or a random accident, so there is no guarantee that you will even be resident on the surface of this world when the large-scale Earth Changes unfold or the Time Blade arrives.

There are some that will say that if large-scale natural disasters and off-world events are meant to cause species extinction on this planet, why should they even make an effort at goodness, virtue, or compassion. We answer them that this is not the only world that your consciousness will ever reside on, and the actions that you engage in during this life do carry onward into the next.

You must know and believe that every action sent outward into the vastness of the great consciousness has an impact— whether that impact is positive or negative.

Things can change in several ways. Should technology take a sudden leap forward, the ability to shield or deflect some of the Time Blade from the larger population centres of the world would allow humankind to maintain a living presence on this world. It would involve quite a lot of compromises in the quality of life that you are willing to endure since the air would be thick with particulate matter for months and perhaps years after the fact. And a great deal of the food sources of the world would disappear in an instant.

Those who survive may not, in the end, wish that they had done so.

What we would hope for you instead is that a percentage of humankind evolves in the way that they were meant to, even if it is at the last moment, and those that evolve can have the knowledge—if they wish—of how to step seamlessly from this world into another one with no pain and no fear.

In an earlier chapter, Deborah has described this method of 'transport' as the opening of a door or gate into another time and space reality. And through diligent spiritual and physical practice, this means of accessing those openings by the spirals and webs of your body's own energy field are available to all of you.

Whether you survive in a form of human body or you step easily back into your more permanent state of soul-body, what legacy do you wish to leave from your time on this world and from your lives to come?

We send blessings to your world and know that you have greater potential for goodness and love than many of you could imagine when you look at the events that are unfolding in your world. Remember that this world is like an out of focus movie projection and that the *real* world lies just beyond the screen which you are observing.

Are you ready for a peek at the other side?

ENDNOTES

[1] Parallel Universes
http://www.bbc.co.uk/science/horizon/2001/parallelunitrans.html

[2] Parallel universe proof boosts time travel hopes
http://www.telegraph.co.uk/science/science-news/3307757/
Parallel-universe-proof-boosts-time-travel-hopes.html

Parallel universes really do exist, according to a mathematical discovery by Oxford scientists that sweeps away one of the key objections to the mind boggling and controversial idea.

The work has wider implications since the idea of parallel universes sidesteps one of the key problems with time travel. Every since it was given serious lab cred in 1949 by the great logician Kurt Godel, many eminent physicists have argued against time travel because it undermines ideas of cause and effect to create paradoxes: a time traveller could go back to kill his grandfather so that he is never born in the first place.

But the existence of parallel worlds offers a way around these troublesome paradoxes, according to David Deutsch of Oxford University, a highly respected proponent of quantum theory, the deeply mathematical, successful and baffling theory of the atomic world.

He argues that time travel shifts between different branches of reality, basing his claim on parallel universes, the so-called "many-worlds" formulation of quantum theory. The new work bolsters his claim that quantum theory does not forbid time travel. "It does sidestep it. You go into another universe," he said yesterday, though he admits that there is still a way to go to find schemes to manipulate space and time in a way that makes time hops possible.

"Many sci fi authors suggested that time travel paradoxes would be solved by parallel universes but in my work, that conclusion is deduced from quantum theory itself", Dr Deutsch said, referring to his work on many worlds. "A motorist who has a near miss, for instance, might feel relieved at his lucky escape. But in a parallel universe, another version of the same driver will have been killed. Yet another universe will see the motorist recover after treatment in hospital. The number of alternative scenarios is endless."

[3] STAR GATE
http://www.fas.org/irp/program/collect/stargate.htm

Over a period of more than two decades some $20 million were spent on STAR GATE and related activities, with $11 million budgeted from the mid-1980's to the early 1990s. Over forty personnel served in the program at various times, including about 23 remote viewers. At its peak during the mid-1980s the program included as many as seven full-time viewers and as many analytical and support personnel. Three psychics were reportedly worked at FT Meade for the CIA from 1990 through July 1995. The psychics were made available to other government agencies which requested their services.

Participants who apparently demonstrated psychic abilities used at least three different techniques at various times:

Coordinate Remote Viewing (CRV) - the original SRI-developed technique in which viewers were asked what they "saw" at specified geographic coordinates.

Extended Remote Viewing (ERV) - a hybrid relaxation/meditative-based method.

Written Remote Viewing (WRV) - a hybrid of both channeling and automatic writing was introduced in 1988, though it proved controversial and was regarded by some as much less reliable.

[4] How Technology May Soon "Read" Your Mind
http://www.cbsnews.com/stories/2008/12/31/60minutes/
main4694713.shtml/?tag=contentMain;contentBody

"I always tell my students that there is no science fiction anymore. All the science fiction I read in high school, we're doing," Paul Root Wolpe, director of the Center for Ethics at Emory University in Atlanta, told Stahl.

To Wolpe, the ability to read our thoughts and intentions this way is revolutionary. "Throughout history, we could never actually coerce someone to reveal information. Torture doesn't work that well, persuasion doesn't work that well. The right to keep one's thoughts locked up in their brain is amongst the most fundamental rights of being human."

"You're saying that if someone can read my intentions, we have to talk about who might in the future be able to do that?" Stahl asked.

"Absolutely," he replied. "Whether we're going to let the state do it or whether we're going to let me do it. I have two teenage daughters. I come home one day and my car is dented and both of them say they didn't do it. Am I going to be allowed to drag them off to the local brain imaging lie detection company and get them put in a scanner? We don't know."

But before we've even started the debate, there are two companies already offering lie detection services using brain scans, one with the catchy name "No Lie MRI." But our experts cautioned that the technique is still unproven.

In the meantime, Haynes is working on something he thinks may be even more effective: reading out from your brain exactly where you've been.

Further into the interview, Wolpe added...

"There are some other technologies that are being developed that may be able to be used covertly and even remotely. So, for example, they're trying to develop now a beam of light that would be projected onto your forehead. It would go a couple of millimeters into your frontal cortex, and then receptors would get the reflection of that light. And there's some studies that suggest that we could use that as a lie detection device," Wolpe said.

He said we wouldn't know if our brains were being scanned. "If you were sitting there in the airport and being questioned, they could beam that on your forehead without your knowledge. We can't do that yet, but they're working on it."

[5] Donald Ewen Cameron
http://www.spartacus.schoolnet.co.uk/JFKcameronDE.htm

Cameron developed the theory that mental patients could be cured by treatment that erased existing memories and by rebuilding the psyche completely. According to his research assistant, Dr. Peter Roper, "He (Cameron) had a technician called Leonard Rubenstein who modified cassettes so there was an endless tape, it could keep repeating itself for hours at a time. If Cameron could give a positive message, eventually a patient would respond to it." Cameron would play the tapes to his patients for up to 86 days, as they slipped in and out of insulin-induced comas.

In the late 1940s Cameron developed a new treatment for mental illness. The authors of Double Standards argue that his "major inspiration was the British psychiatrist William Sargent, whom Cameron considered to be the leading expert on Soviet brainwashing techniques. Cameron took this work and used it for what he called' 'depatterning'. He believed that after inducing complete amnesia in a patient, he could then selectively recover their memory in such a way as to change their behaviour unrecognisably."

In 1953 Cameron developed what he called "psychic driving". Cameron developed the theory that mental patients could be cured by treatment that erased existing memories and by rebuilding the psyche completely. According to his research assistant, Dr. Peter Roper, "He (Cameron) had a technician called Leonard Rubenstein who modified cassettes so there was an endless tape, it could keep repeating itself for hours at a time. If Cameron could give a positive message, eventually a patient would respond to it." Cameron would play the tapes to his patients for up to 86 days, as they slipped in and out of insulin-induced comas.

Cameron discovered that "once a subject entered an amnesiac, somnambulistic state, they would become hypersensitive to suggestion". In other words they could be brainwashed. The CIA became aware of Cameron's research and in 1957 Cameron was recruited by Allen Dulles, Director of the CIA, to run Project MKULTRA. Documents released in 1977 show that MKULTRA was a "mind control" program. As it was illegal for the CIA to conduct operations on American soil, Cameron was forced to carry out his experiments at the Allan Memorial Institute in Canada. The CIA arranged funding via Cornell University in New York.

[6] Air Force report calls for $7.5M to study psychic teleportation

"Star Trek/ fans may be happy to hear that the Air Force has paid to study psychic teleportation. But scientists aren't so thrilled. The Air Force Research Lab's August "Teleportation Physics Report," posted earlier this week on the Federation of American Scientists (FAS) Web site, struck a raw nerve with physicists and critics of wasteful military spending. In the report, author Eric Davis says psychic teleportation, moving yourself from location to location through mind powers, is "quite real and can be controlled."

The 88-page report also reviews a range of teleportation concepts and experiments: Quantum teleportation, a technique demonstrated in the last decade that shifts the characteristics, but not the location, of sub-atomic particles at great distances.

Wormholes, a highly theoretical possibility whereby the intense gravitational field near black holes could rip open entrances to distant locales.

The report calls for $7.5 million to conduct psychic teleportation experiments.

"The views expressed in the report are those of the author and do not necessarily reflect the official policy of the Air Force, the Department of Defense or the U.S. Government," says an

Air Force Research Lab (AFRL) statement sent to USA TODAY. "There are no plans by the AFRL Propulsion Directorate for additional funding on this contract." Explaining why the lab sponsored the study, AFRL spokesman Ranney Adams said, "If we don't turn over stones, we don't know if we have missed something."
USATODAY 11/05/04: by Dan Vergano

[7] Psychic Spy: The Story of an Astounding Man
http://www.reuters.com/article/pressRelease/idUS136095+21-Apr-2009+PRN20090421
Published by Doubleday; Dr.Ernesto Moshe Montgomery

[8] The Complete User's Manual For Coordinate Remote Viewing by Dr. David Morehouse
Publisher: Sounds True, Incorporated (November 1, 2007), ISBN-13: 978-1591792390

[9] Unholy Alliance: A History of Nazi Involvement with the Occult by Peter Levenda - page 32, Published by The Continuum International Publishing Group, Inc., New York, NY 2007

[10] Ibid, page 231

[11] Ibid, page 230

[12] Is This Cow A Human-Animal Hybrid?
http://seedmagazine.com/content/article/is_this_cow_a_human-animal_hybrid/

A Dutch biotechnology company called Pharming has genetically engineered cows, outfitting females with a human gene that causes them to express high levels of the protein human lactoferrin in their milk. According to Pharming's website,"the protein, which is naturally present in human tears, lung secretions, milk and other bodily fluids, fights against the bacteria that causes eye and lung infections, plays a key role in the immune system of infants and adults and improves intestinal microbial balance, promoting the health of the gastro-intestinal tract. Since the protein has the ability to bind iron, is a natural anti-bacterial, anti-fungal and anti-viral, is an antioxidant and also has immunomodulatory properties, large groups of people might benefit from orally administered lactoferrin," the company literature reads.

Scientists have tested the toxicity of the protein isolated from the cows' milk on rats. They found that even at the high level of 2,000 mg recombinant human lactoferrin per kg body weight orally consumed human lactoferrin has no adverse effects to complement all the supposed benefits already mentioned. Pharming has, therefore, filed a notification with the FDA asking that their lactoferrin be labeled' 'Generally Recognized As Safe' (GRAS). If the FDA approves this product, human lactoferrin derived from these cloned cows could be in America's yogurt, popsicles, sports drinks and snack bars within months.

To create human lactoferrin-lactating cows, Pharming's scientists introduce human DNA coding for the protein's production into the nuclei of fertilized bovine eggs. The cells that successfully incorporate the foreign DNA or' 'transgene' are then selected, and each is fused with a second egg cell that has had its nucleus removed. The fused cells are then implanted in a surrogate cow's uterus. If all goes well, the cow becomes pregnant with a transgenic calf that, upon maturity two years later, will produce milk containing human lactoferrin. Despite that one component of its milk, the calf is all bovine, but technically remains an example of the dastardly human-animal hybrid.

"We believe that the benefit with our product is that it is a human protein, as opposed to a protein that is of animal origin," said Singh, explaining why Pharming is going through the trouble of recombining DNA. "So, because it's a human protein, it will interact with the human receptors in the gastrointestinal tract."

The' 'humanness' of the protein may be both its strongest selling point and the label that will delay and possibly squash its eventual release to the marketplace. Surveys consistently show that Americans are wary of using genetically modified animals, specifically cloned animals, for food. In fact, a 2005 survey by the Pew Initiative On Food And Biotechnology found that only 23% of American consumers believe that food from cloned animals is safe, while 43% believe it is unsafe.

[13] UK's first hybrid embryos created
http://news.bbc.co.uk/go/pr/fr/-/2/hi/health/7323298.stm
By Fergus Walsh: Medical correspondent, BBC News

Scientists at Newcastle University have created part-human, part-animal hybrid embryos for the first time in the UK, the BBC can reveal.

The embryos survived for up to three days and are part of medical research into a range of illnesses.

The Catholic Church describes it as "monstrous". But medical bodies and patient groups say such research is vital for our understanding of disease. They argue that the work could pave the way for new treatments for conditions such as Parkinson's and Alzheimer's.

Egg shortages

Under the microscope the round bundles of cells look like any other three-day-old embryos. In fact they are hybrids - part-human, part-animal. "We are dealing with a clump of cells which would never go on to develop " John Burn-Newcastle University.

They were created by injecting DNA derived from human skin cells into eggs taken from cows ovaries which have had virtually all their genetic material removed. The Newcastle team say they are using cow ovaries because human eggs from donors are a precious resource and in short supply.

The article continues and states that —

The hybrid embryos are purely for research and would never be allowed to develop beyond 14 days when they are still smaller than a pinhead.

Scientists want to extract stem cells, the body's master cells, from the embryos, in order to increase understanding of a whole range of diseases from diabetes to stroke and ultimately to produce treatments.

But not all of the scientists who were contacted for commentary by the author of this article agree with the assertions of Newcastle University. Dr David King, of Human Genetics Alert, said: "For anyone who understands basic biology, it is no surprise that these embryos died at such an early stage. Cloning is inefficient precisely because it is so unnatural, and by mixing species it becomes even more unnatural and unlikely to succeed."

"The public has been grossly misled by the hype that this is vital medical research. Even if stem cells were ever to be produced, like cloned animals, they would have so many errors of their metabolism that they would produce completely misleading data."

Published: 2008/04/0

14 Could We Create Quantum Creatures In The Lab
http://www.newscientist.com/article/dn17792-could-we-create-quantum-creatures-in-the-lab.html

Quantum weirdness could soon invade the living world, if a scheme to give a flu virus a strange double life comes off.

In quantum theory, a single object can be doing two different things at once. This so-called "superposition" is a delicate state, destroyed by any contact with the outside world. The largest objects that have been superposed so far are molecules. It is hard to put a much larger object such as a cat or human into a superposition because air molecules and photons are always bouncing off it.

But it might be possible with a small life form, according to Oriol Romero-Isart of the Max Planck Institute for Quantum Optics in Garching, Germany, and his colleagues. They hope to prove the concept with the flu virus, which exhibits some properties of life, because it can survive in a vacuum — solving the problem of pesky air molecules.

[15] GMO Foods

http://www.aaemonline.org/gmopost.html

A May 2009 report by the American Academy of Environmental Health states...

Therefore, because GM foods pose a serious health risk in the areas of toxicology, allergy and immune function, reproductive health, and metabolic, physiologic and genetic health and are without benefit, the AAEM believes that it is imperative to adopt the precautionary principle, which is one of the main regulatory tools of the European Union environmental and health policy and serves as a foundation for several international agreements. The most commonly used definition is from the 1992 Rio Declaration that states: "In order to protect the environment, the precautionary approach shall be widely applied by States according to their capabilities. Where there are threats of serious or irreversible damage, lack of full scientific certainty shall not be used as a reason for postponing cost-effective measures to prevent environmental degradation.

Another often used definition originated from an environmental meeting in the United States in 1998 stating: "When an activity raises threats to the environment or human health, precautionary measures should be taken, even if some cause and effect relationships are not fully established scientifically. In this context, the proponent of an activity, rather than the public, should bear the burden of proof (of the safety of the activity).

[16] GMO Regulation

http://www.aaemonline.org/gmopost.html

[17] Virus Detection Via Chip

http://www.reuters.com/article/hotStocksNews/
idUSTRE58K4BZ20090921

(Reuters) - Shares of VeriChip Corp (CHIP.O) tripled after the company said it had been granted an exclusive license to two patents, which will help it to develop implantable virus detection systems in humans.

The patents, held by VeriChip partner Receptors LLC, relate to biosensors that can detect the H1N1 and other viruses, and biological threats such as methicillin-resistant Staphylococcus aureus, VeriChip said in a statement.

The technology will combine with VeriChip's implantable radio frequency identification devices to develop virus triage detection systems.

[18] Microchip Implant to Link Your Health Records, Credit History, Social Security
http://industry.bnet.com/pharma/10004616/microchip-implant-to-link-your-health-records-credit-history-social-security/

[19] Origins of H1N1 Virus
http://www.waynemadsenreport.com/
From an article in the Wayne Madson Report,

It has also been discovered that suspected ancestor viruses are coming from old isolates. The NA gene comes from a 1996-2001 isolate, the M gene from 1990-1993 isolates, and the others even older, somewhere between 1979 to 1980s isolates. The consensus virologist community contends that the A/H1N1 virus has been in existence for over 20 years without ever being detected. WMR's virologist states that it is impossible for a virus existing for 20 years without being detected given the amount of virus medical surveillance that takes place around the world.

The virologist has not detected any evidence of 1918 influenza RNA/DNA in A/H1N1. However, the 1918 flu, like A/H1N1, began in a first wave in the spring and came back with a vengeance in October. The 1918 flu killed an estimated 50 million people around the world. Although no genetic evidence of a link to 1918 flu has been discovered by the virologist, the same scientist who has conducted research into A/H1N1 and may have received DNA samples from the buried corpse of an Inuit woman in Fort Brevig, Alaska, who died of the pandemic in 1918 is also financially linked to an A/H1N1 vaccine firm.

The virologist has asked an alarming question about A/H1N1,"How can you mix avian, human and pig virus at one time? The viruses must have come from Europe, America and Asia, without any detection?"

The virologist adds, "The virus emerged suddenly in Mexico. I can't explain how. I wish I could. For me as a virologist, it's impossible . . . on the other hand, technology can create any kind of virus you want."

[20] GMO's Enable Trojan Horse Vaccinations
http://www.naturalnews.com/026434_vaccines_vaccination_vaccinations.html

Edible vaccines, as GMO foods, are in the future as well. Meat and Poultry, a business journal for meat and poultry processors, reports in a May 5, 2009 article, by Bryan Salvage, that researchers at Iowa State University are working on creating a method to install vaccines into corn crops.

"We're trying to figure out which genes from the swine influenza virus to incorporate into corn", stated Hank Harris, a researcher on the project. "If a swine flu virus breaks out, the corn could be shipped to the location to try to vaccinate animals and humans in the area quickly. . . . there is no need for extensive vaccine purification, which can be an expensive process."

This way even corn products, including corn chips and corn syrup, which is ubiquitous in processed foods, can serve as vaccination vehicles for humans while the corn itself is fed to hogs. Starting in 1996, bananas have been considered as a vaccination vehicle for developing countries. Keep in mind that this will be genetically engineered, or GMO (genetically modified organisms), so you won't know where and when it will show up on the food shelves.

[21] US Army Toyed With Telepathic Ray Gun
http://technology.newscientist.com/channel/tech/dn13513-us-army-toyed-with-telepathic-ray-gun.html?feedId=online-news_rss20

A recently declassified US Army report on the biological effects of non-lethal weapons reveals outlandish plans for "ray gun" devices, which would cause artificial fevers or beam voices into people's heads.

The report titled "Bioeffects Of Selected Nonlethal Weapons" was released under the US Freedom of Information Act and is available on this website (pdf). The DoD has confirmed to New Scientist that it released the documents, which detail five different "maturing non-lethal technologies" using microwaves, lasers and sound.

Released by US Army Intelligence and Security Command at Fort Meade, Maryland, US, the 1998 report gives an overview of what was then the state of the art in directed energy weapons for crowd control and other applications.

A word in your ear

Some of the technologies are conceptual, such as an electro-magnetic pulse that causes a seizure like those experienced by people with epilepsy. Other ideas, like a microwave gun to "beam" words directly into people's ears, have been tested. It is claimed that the so-called "Frey Effect" - using close-range microwaves to produce audible sounds in a person's ears Đ has been used to project the spoken numbers 1 to 10 across a lab to volunteers'.

In 2004 the US Navy funded research into using the Frey effect to project sound that caused "discomfort" into the ears of crowds.

The report also discusses a microwave weapon able to produce a disabling "artificial fever" by heating a person's body. While tests of the idea are not mentioned, the report notes that the necessary equipment "is available today". It adds that while it would take at least fifteen minutes to achieve the desired "fever" effect, it could be used to incapacitate people for almost "any desired period consistent with safety."

Less exotic technologies discussed include laser dazzlers and a sound source loud enough to disturb the sense of balance. Both have been realised in the years since the report was written. The US army uses laser dazzlers in Iraq, while the Long Range Acoustic Device has military and civilian users, and has been used on one occasion to repel pirates off Somalia.

Potentially torturous

Steve Wright, a security expert at Leeds Metropolitan University, UK, warns that the technologies described could be used for torture. In 1998 the European Parliament passed a motion banning potentially dangerous incapacitating technologies that interfere with the human brain.

"The epileptic seizure inducing device is grossly irresponsible and should never be fielded," says Steve Wright "We know from similar [chemically] artificially-induced fits that the victim subsequently remains "potentiated" and may spontaneously suffer epileptic fits again after the initial attack."

The acoustic energy device that affects the ear canals, disrupting the motion sense, may require dangerously loud sound levels to be effective, points out Juergen Altmann, a physicist at Dortmund University, Germany, who is interested in new military technologies.

"[There is] inconsistency between the part that says "interesting" effects occur at 130-155 dB and the Recovery/ Safety section that says that 115 dB is to be avoided - without commenting on the difference."

[22] Airline Shock Bracelets
http://amsam.org/2008/03/air-safety-proposal-shock-bracelets.html

Lamperd, a' 'firearm training system' company, has patented a bracelet that delivers debilitating shocks when remotely triggered [by an airline attendant, air marshal or the pilot]. They are proposing that the TSA [the U.S.A's Transportation Safety Administration] could force everyone who flies to wear one of these and then flight-attendants could zap passengers into a stupor if they turn out to be terrorists.

A method of providing air travel security for passengers traveling via an aircraft comprises situating a remotely activatable electric shock device on each of the passengers in position to deliver a disabling electrical shock when activated; and arming the electric shock devices for subsequent selective activation by a selectively

operable remote control disposed within the aircraft. The remotely activatable electric shock devices each have activation circuitry responsive to the activating signal transmitted from the selectively operable remote control means. The activated electric shock device is operable to deliver the disabling electrical shock to that passenger.

[23] Packs of Robots Will Hunt Down Uncooperative Humans http://www.newscientist.com/blogs/shortsharpscience/200 8/10/packs-of-robots-will-hunt-down.html?DCMP=ILC-hmts&nsref=specrt10_head_Pack%20hunting%20robots

The latest request from the Pentagon jars the senses. At least, it did mine. They are looking for contractors to provide a "Multi-Robot Pursuit System" that will let packs of robots "search for and detect a non-cooperative human". Given that iRobot last year struck a deal with Taser International to mount stun weapons on its military robots, how long before we see packs of droids hunting down pesky demonstrators with paralysing weapons?

Steve Wright of Leeds Metropolitan University is an expert on police and military technologies, and last year correctly predicted this pack-hunting mode of operation would happen. "The giveaway here is the phrase' 'a non-cooperative human subject'," he told me: "What we have here are the beginnings of something designed to enable robots to hunt down humans like a pack of dogs. Once the software is perfected we can reasonably anticipate that they will become autonomous and become armed.

We can also expect such systems to be equipped with human detection and tracking devices including sensors which detect human breath and the radio waves associated with a human heart beat. These are technologies already developed."

Another commentator often in the news for his views on military robot autonomy is Noel Sharkey, an AI and robotics engineer at the University of Sheffield. He says he can understand why the military want such technology, but also worries it will be used irresponsibly. "This is a clear step towards one of the main goals of the US Army's Future Combat Systems project, which aims to make a single soldier the nexus for a large scale robot attack. Independently, ground and aerial robots have been tested together and once the bits are joined, there will be a robot force under command of a single soldier with potentially dire consequences for innocents around the corner."

[24] Dragonfly or Insect Spy? Scientists at Work on Robobugs
By Rick Weiss- *Washington Post* Staff Writer
http://www.washingtonpost.com/wp-dyn/content/
article/2007/10/08/AR2007100801434_pf.html

Vanessa Alarcon saw them while working at an antiwar rally in Lafayette Square last month. "I heard someone say,' 'Oh my god, look at those,' "the college senior from New York recalled. "I look up and I'm like,' 'What the hell is that?' They looked kind of like dragonflies or little helicopters. But I mean, those are not insects."

Out in the crowd, Bernard Crane saw them, too. "I'd never seen anything like it in my life," the Washington lawyer said. "They were large for dragonflies. I thought,' 'Is that mechanical, or is that alive?' "

That is just one of the questions hovering over a handful of similar sightings at political events in Washington and New York. Some suspect the insectlike drones are high-tech surveillance tools, perhaps deployed by the Department of Homeland Security.

Others think they are, well, dragonflies—an ancient order of insects that even biologists concede look about as robotic as a living creature can look.

No agency admits to having deployed insect-size spy drones. But a number of U.S. government and private entities acknowledge they are trying. Some federally funded teams are even growing live insects with computer chips in them, with the goal of mounting spyware on their bodies and controlling their flight muscles remotely.

[25] Climate Change May Trigger Earthquakes and Volcanoes
http://www.newscientist.com/article/mg20327273.800-climate-change-may-trigger-earthquakes-and-volcanoes.html

Far from being the benign figure of mythology, Mother Earth is short-tempered and volatile. So sensitive in fact, that even slight changes in weather and climate can rip the planet's crust apart, unleashing the furious might of volcanic eruptions, earthquakes and landslides.

That's the conclusion of the researchers who got together last week in London at the conference on Climate Forcing of Geological and Geomorphological Hazards. It suggests climate change could tip the planet's delicate balance and unleash a host of geological disasters. What's more, even our attempts to stall global warming could trigger a catastrophic event.

Fisher continues, saying —

Small ocean changes can also influence volcanic eruptions, says David Pyle of the University of Oxford. His study of eruptions over the past 300 years with Ben Mason of the University of Cambridge and colleagues reveals that volcanism varies with the seasons. The team found that there are around 20 per cent more eruptions worldwide during the northern hemisphere's winter than the summer (Journal of Geophysical Research, DOI: 10.1029/2002JB002293). The reason may be that global sea level drops slightly during the northern hemisphere's winter. Because there is more land in the northern hemisphere, more water is locked up as ice and snow on land than during the southern hemisphere's winter.

The vast majority of the world's most active volcanoes are within a few tens of kilometres of the coast (see map). This suggests the seasonal removal of some of the ocean's weight at continental margins as sea level drops could be triggering eruptions around the world, says Pyle.

And what if the so-called solutions for the problems of Climate Change are actually just as likely to create additional damage as doing nothing. Fisher examines this dilemma when he reveals...

It all looked so promising - tidy carbon dioxide away underground and forget about it. But even as the US's first large-scale sequestration operation is getting off the ground at the Mountaineer plant in West Virginia, geophysicists are concerned that burying the carbon could trigger earthquakes and tsunamis.

In a carbon sequestration power plant (CCS), CO_2 is extracted from the exhaust then pumped into aquifers and old gas fields several kilometres beneath the Earth's surface. So far so good. But the CO_2 expands as it rises through the porous rock, increasing pressure inside. "If enough CO_2 is injected into an aquifer, it could increase the pressure enough to reactivate a fault and trigger an earthquake," warns Andrew Chadwick of the British Geological Survey.

Chemical reactions between the injected CO_2, water and rock could also destabilise the rock, says Ernest Majer, a seismologist at the Lawrence Berkeley National Laboratory in California who briefed the Senate on CCS hazards this week. "It's such a new technology that none of these issues have been addressed," says Majer. Even storage sites far from human settlements could have disastrous effects, warns Christian Klose, a geophysicist at the Think Geohazards consulting firm in California. A CCS facility at the Sleipner gas field in the North Sea, may have triggered a magnitude 4 earthquake in 2008. Had it been bigger, says Klose, it might have triggered a tsunami.

[26] Asteroid Impact Fueled Global Rain of BBs
http://www.space.com/scienceastronomy/050328_asteroid_impact.html

The asteroid that struck the Yucatan Peninsula 65 million years ago presumably initiated the extinction of the dinosaurs. The huge collision also unleashed a worldwide downpour of tiny BB-sized mineral droplets, called spherules.

The hard rain did not pelt the dinosaurs to death. But the planet-covering residue left behind may tell us something about the direction of the incoming asteroid, as well as possible extinction scenarios, according to new research. The falling spherules might have heated the atmosphere enough to start a global fire, as one example.

How the spherules formed in the first place, though, has been a bit of a mystery. One theory is that these half-millimeter-wide globules precipitated out of a giant cloud of vaporized rock that circled the planet after the collision.

"That vapor is very hot and expands outward from the point of impact, cooling and expanding as it goes," said Lawrence Grossman of the University of Chicago. "As it cools the vapor condenses as little droplets and rains out over the whole Earth."

Grossman and Denton Ebel, from the American Museum of Natural History, have shown that this vapor condensation model is consistent with data taken from spherules around the world.

The scientists also found that chemical differences in spherules from the Atlantic and Pacific Ocean imply that the vapor plume initially moved east, which might pinpoint the arrival direction of the asteroid.

Apocalyptic fireball

The spherules populate a three-millimeter layer, called the K-T boundary, which separates the Cretaceous from the Paleogene (formally called the Tertiary) geologic periods. The abrupt disappearance of dinosaur fossils — as well as many marine life fossils — above this boundary implies a major extinction event occurred 65 million years ago.

Around this same time, a city-sized asteroid landed near the present-day town of Chicxulub, Mexico, where traces of a 100-mile-wide crater can still be found.

There is evidence for the asteroid in the unique mineral content of the KT boundary — specifically a high concentration of iridium. This heavy element is very rare on the Earth's surface but is found in high quantities in meteorites.

The implication is that the energy released in the collision fueled a fireball of vaporized rock that rose above the clouds. In this way the asteroid's contents — as well as the material at the crash site — were dispersed across the globe.

[27] EXCERPT: 109TH CONGRESS—1ST SESSION H. R. 1022 http://science.house.gov/Publications/hearings_markups_details. aspx?NewsID=2033

To provide for a Near-Earth Object Survey program to detect, track, catalogue, and characterize certain near-earth asteroids and comets.

IN THE HOUSE OF REPRESENTATIVES

MARCH 1, 2005

Mr. ROHRABACHER (for himself, Mr. NADLER, and Mr. WEINER) introduced the following bill; which was referred to the Committee on Science. A BILL To provide for a Near-Earth Object Survey program to detect, track, catalogue, and characterize certain near-earth asteroids and comets. Be it enacted by the Senate and House of Representatives of the United States of America in Congress assembled,

SECTION 1. SHORT TITLE.

This Act may be cited as the "George E. Brown, Jr. Near-Earth Object Survey Act".

SEC. 2. FINDINGS.

The Congress makes the following findings:

(1) Near-Earth objects pose a serious and credible threat to humankind, as scientists are certain that a major asteroid or comet was responsible for the mass extinction of the majority of the Earth's species, including the dinosaurs, nearly 65,000,000 years ago.

(2) Similar objects have struck the Earth or passed through the Earth's atmosphere several times in the Earth's history and pose a similar threat in the future.

(3) Several such near-Earth objects have only been discovered within days of the objects' closest approach to Earth, and recent discoveries of such large objects indicate that many large near-Earth objects remain undiscovered.

(4) The efforts taken to date by the National Aeronautics and Space Administration for detecting and characterizing the hazards of Earth orbit-crossing asteroids and comets are not sufficient to the threat posed by such objects to cause widespread destruction and loss of life.

SEC. 3. DEFINITION.

For purposes of this Act, the term "Administrator" means the Administrator of the National Aeronautics and Space Administration.

SEC. 4. NEAR-EARTH OBJECT SURVEY.

(a) SURVEY PROGRAM. The Administrator shall plan, develop, and implement a Near-Earth Object Survey program to detect, track, catalogue, and characterize the physical characteristics of near-Earth asteroids and comets equal to or greater than 100 meters in diameter in order to assess the threat of such near-Earth objects in striking the Earth.

[28] Deep Impact
http://www.nasa.gov/deepimpact

Deep Impact is comprised of two parts, a flyby spacecraft and a smaller impactor. The impactor will be released into the comet's path for the planned high-speed collision. The crater produced by the impactor is expected to range from the width of a house up to the size of a football stadium and be from two to 14 stories deep. Ice and dust debris will be ejected from the crater revealing the material beneath.

Along with the imagers aboard Deep Impact, NASA's Hubble, Spitzer and Chandra space telescopes, along with the largest telescopes on Earth, will observe the effects of the material flying from the comet's newly formed crater.

An intimate glimpse beneath the surface of a comet, where material and debris from the formation of the solar system remain relatively unchanged, will answer basic questions about the how the solar system formed. The effects of the collision will offer a better look at the nature and composition of these celestial travelers.

Principal Investigator A'Hearn leads the mission from the University of Maryland, College Park. JPL manages the Deep Impact project for the Science Mission Directorate at NASA Headquarters. Deep Impact is a mission in NASA's Discovery Program of moderately priced solar system exploration missions. Ê The spacecraft was built for NASA by Ball Aerospace & Technologies Corporation, Boulder, Colorado.

[29] Warning Over Stealth Comets
http://independent.co.uk/news/science/warning-over-stealth-comets-531735.html

Comets that are invisible to astronomers could pose a lethal threat from space, scientists said yesterday. They believe that giant "stealth" comets made up of loose material reflect so little light that they cannot be seen. If the theory is right, the chance of the Earth being hit by a comet big enough to wipe out human civilisation may be higher than experts believe.

Professor Chandra Wickramasinghe, head of the team at Cardiff University's Centre for Astrobiology, which delivered the warning, said: "It's possible we need to think again about mitigating strategies."

The Cardiff scientists found the surfaces of inactive comets composed of loose, organic material develop such small reflectivities that they are invisible.

Fortunately, the American space agency Nasa has a new weapon with the power to "de-cloak" stealth comets, the professor said. The £115m Widefield Infrared Survey Explorer, to be launched in 2008, will scan the sky for cool failed stars called brown dwarfs, clouds of space dust and faraway galaxies. It is up to 500,000 times more sensitive than previous telescopes.

[30] Asteroid attack: Putting Earth's defences to the test —
23 September 2009
http://www.newscientist.com/article/mg20327271.300-asteroid-attack-putting-earths-defences-to-the-test.html

...the US air force recently brought together scientists, military officers and emergency-response officials for the first time to assess the nation's ability to cope, should it come to pass.

The exercise, which took place in December 2008, exposed the chilling dangers asteroids pose. Not only is there no plan for what to do when an asteroid hits, but our early-warning systems - which could make the difference between life and death - are woefully inadequate. The meeting provided just the wake-up call organiser Peter Garreston had hoped to create. He has long been concerned about the threat of an impact. "As a taxpayer, I would appreciate my air force taking a look at something that would be certainly as bad as nuclear terrorism in a city, and potentially a civilisation-ending event," he says.

And further into the article...

If you were unfortunate enough to be looking up from directly below, the explosion would be brighter than the sun. The visible and infrared radiation would be strong enough to make anything flammable ignite, says Mark Boslough of Sandia National Laboratory in Livermore, California. "It's like being in a broiler oven," he says. Anyone directly exposed would quickly be very badly burned.

Even before the sound of the blast reaches you, your body would be smashed by a devastating supersonic shock wave as the explosion creates a bubble of high-pressure air that expands faster than the speed of sound.

[31] NASA Plans Lunar Outpost: Permanent Base at Moon's South Pole Envisioned by 2024
http://www.washingtonpost.com/wp-dyn/content/
article/2006/12/04/AR2006120400837.html
Marc Kaufman: *Washington Post* Staff Writer-Tuesday, December 5, 2006

NASA unveiled plans yesterday to set up a small and ultimately self-sustaining settlement of astronauts at the south pole of the moon sometime around 2020 — the first step in an ambitious plan to resume manned exploration of the solar system.

The long-awaited proposal envisions initial stays of a week by four-person crews, followed by gradually longer visits until power and other supplies are in place to make a permanent presence possible by 2024.

The effort was presented as an unprecedented mission to learn about the moon and places beyond, as well as an integral part of a long-range plan to send astronauts to Mars. The moon settlement would ultimately be a way station for space travelers headed onward, and would provide not only a haven but also hydrogen and oxygen mined from the lunar surface to make water and rocket fuel.

NASA Deputy Administrator Shana Dale said the agency met with hundreds of scientists, potential international partners and space businesses over the past year to discuss lunar options — most pressingly, whether the plan should be based around a series of sorties to the moon or a permanent outpost and later settlement. The conclusion, she said, was that an outpost would be the best both for science and to prepare for exploration deeper into space.

Scott Horowitz, chief of lunar exploration, said: "The lunar base will be a central theme in our going forward plan for going back to the moon in preparation to go to Mars and beyond. It's a very, very big decision, and it's one of the few where I've seen the scientific community and the engineering community actually agree on anything."

Dale said that once the team endorsed the concept of an outpost, which would be about the size of the Mall, the next debate was over where to put it, with a focus on either of the moon's poles.

"Conditions at the south pole appear to be more moderate and safer," she said. The south pole is almost constantly bathed in light and would be an ideal place to set up solar-power collectors for an electrical system — a precondition for achieving the kind of "living off the land" that NASA is aiming for.

Horowitz also said the polar sites are scientifically exciting because "we don't know as much about the lunar poles as we know about Mars." Officials said the area around the south pole has craters that probably hold volatile gases that could be collected for commercial purposes. Highest on the list of possible resources is helium-3, a form of the gas seldom found on Earth that could be well suited for nuclear power fuel.

The rockets and space capsules that will take astronauts back to the moon will be exclusively American, but Dale said the mission envisions and needs the cooperation of other nations. As part of the process, she said, NASA officials met with representatives from the European Space Agency and the national space agencies of Australia, Britain, Canada, China, France, Germany, India, Italy, Russia, South Korea and Ukraine.

Dale said she will travel extensively next year to these nations and others to see how they might participate. One project she mentioned as attractive to NASA and possibly others is the deployment of an array of telescopes on the dark side of the moon to see far into the universe.

The NASA plan grew out of President Bush's Vision for Space Exploration, which was announced in 2004 and calls for sending astronauts back to the moon and later to Mars. Congress almost unanimously embraced the general plan last year in an authorization bill, but questions remain about its funding. NASA is counting on redirecting billions of dollars from the space shuttle and international space station programs to fund development of a new spaceship, but some critics have complained that the agency is already cutting back its science programs to pay for the moon-Mars project.

[32] New' 'super-Earth' found in space
http://news.bbc.co.uk/2/hi/science/nature/6589157.stm

Astronomers have found the most Earth-like planet outside our Solar System to date, a world which could have water running on its surface. The planet orbits the faint star Gliese 581, which is 20.5 light-years away in the constellation Libra. Scientists made the discovery using the Eso 3.6m Telescope in Chile. They say the benign temperatures on the planet mean any water there could exist in liquid form, and this raises the chances it could also harbour life.

"We have estimated that the mean temperature of this' 'super-Earth' lies between 0 and 40 degrees Celsius, and water would thus be liquid," explained Stephane Udry of the Geneva Observatory, lead author of the scientific paper reporting the result. "Moreover, its radius should be only 1.5 times the Earth's radius, and models predict that the planet should be either rocky - like our Earth - or covered with oceans."

Xavier Delfosse, a member of the team from Grenoble University, added: "Liquid water is critical to life as we know it." He believes the planet may now become a very important target for future space missions dedicated to the search for extra-terrestrial life.

These missions will put telescopes in space that can discern the tell-tale light "signatures" that might be associated with biological processes. The observatories would seek to identify trace atmospheric gases such as methane, and even markers for chlorophyll, the pigment in Earth plants that plays a critical role in photosynthesis.

'Indirect' detection

The exoplanet - as astronomers call planets around a star other than the Sun - is the smallest yet found, and has been given the designation Gliese 581 c. It completes a full orbit of its parent star in just 13 days.

EXOPLANET GLIESE 581 C

Mass: Five times Earth's mass

Orbit: 13 days

Temperature: 0C - 40C

Distance: 20.5 light years

Constellation: Libra

Indeed, it is 14 times closer to its star than the Earth is to our Sun. However, given that the host star is smaller and colder than the Sun - and thus less luminous - the planet nevertheless lies in the "habitable zone", the region around a star where water could be liquid.

Gliese 581 c was identified at the European Southern Observatory (Eso) facility at La Silla in the Atacama Desert. To make their discovery, researchers used a very sensitive instrument that can measure tiny changes in the velocity of a star as it experiences the gravitational tug of a nearby planet. Astronomers are stuck with such indirect methods of detection because current telescope technology struggles to image very distant and faint objects - especially when they orbit close to the glare of a star.

The Gliese 581 system has now yielded three planets: the new super-Earth, a 15 Earth-mass planet (Gliese 581 b) orbiting even closer to the parent star, and an eight Earth-mass planet that lies further out (Gliese 581 d).

The latest discovery has created tremendous excitement among scientists. Of the more than 200 exoplanets so far discovered, a great many are Jupiter-like gas giants that experience blazing temperatures because they orbit close in to much hotter stars.

The Gliese 581 super-Earth is in what scientists also sometimes call the "Goldilocks Zone", where temperatures "are just right" for life to have a chance to exist.

Commenting on the discovery, Alison Boyle, the curator of astronomy at London's Science Museum, said: "Of all the planets we've found around other stars, this is the one that looks as though it might have the right ingredients for life. "It's 20 light-years away and so we won't be going there anytime soon, but with new kinds of propulsion technology that could change in the future. And obviously we'll be training some powerful telescopes on it to see what we can see," she told BBC News.

"'Is there life anywhere else?' is a fundamental question we all ask."

Professor Glenn White at the Rutherford Appleton Laboratory is helping to develop the European Space Agency's Darwin mission, which will scan the nearby Universe, looking for signs of life on Earth-like planets. He said: "This is an important step in the search for true Earth-like exoplanets. "As the methods become more and more refined, astronomers are narrowing in on the ultimate goal - the detection of a true Earth-like planet elsewhere. Obviously this newly discovered planet and its companions in the Gliese 581 system will become prominent targets for missions like Esa's Darwin and Nasa's Terrestrial planet Finder when they fly in about a decade."

The discovery is reported in the journal Astronomy & Astrophysics.

CONTACT INFORMATION

Email
Deborah Harmes, Ph.D.
dkhthedreamkeeper@yahoo.com.au

Websites
Multiversal Musing—My frequently updated blog
http://www.multiversalmusing.com

Deborah Harmes, Ph.D.
The gateway site for all my updated
information on books and lectures
http://www.deborahharmes.com

www.ingramcontent.com/pod-product-compliance
Lightning Source LLC
Chambersburg PA
CBHW021233090426
42740CB00006B/517